# THAD
# HAYES

# THAD HAYES

*the*
Tailored Interior

RIZZOLI
NEW YORK

CONTENTS

It's about time. It's about time that a book showing the work of the wonderful interior designer Thad Hayes can be shared with readers interested in what distinguishes a great interior designer from a merely good one.

Designers can be formulaic; they can leave *their* stamp on a room, almost literally putting their name in the room, leaving the client in an anonymous abyss. Not so with Thad Hayes.

With his Southern charm and easy smile, Thad listens intently to his client and produces rooms that don't need to be changed, since they reflect their owner so well.

In these beautiful pages you will see how Thad's use of proportion and scale invites people into a room.

For my husband, Leonard, and me, Thad created an Adirondack masterpiece in our country home, a tiny one-bedroom log cabin near a pond. Thad filled this home with twig furniture and handcrafted lamps, tables, and bookcases. Now, a favorite hideaway is loaded with charm, color, and patterns, creating the perfect weekend getaway.

In Florida, Thad reworked a formal Georgian house completed in 1938 into our elegant but practical beach house. Since the house literally sits on the beach, Thad chose to keep it elegant without using fancy silks or overly delicate materials. Instead he employed straw rugs on the first floor, anticipating the return from an ocean swim by our guests with sand between their toes. Linens, cottons, and cotton blends with a crisp, smooth hand in elegant, cool colors give our formal rooms the right look, but one could sit on any chair in the breakfast room or dining room in a damp bathing suit.

Touches of extravagance are suggested in Lalique fixtures, Ruhlmann sconces, Chareau chairs, art deco mirrors, and the massing of Leonard's art deco posters on one wall in the media room. These touches, appropriate and contemporary to the era of the house, feel as if they had been there from the time the house was built. Thad's restoration even earned a commendation from the Preservation Foundation of Palm Beach.

In other words, Thad Hayes can make a home fit into *its* own skin, not into his skin.

And, he is nice. The relationship with a client is key to Thad. After all, sometimes fabrics need to be changed, lampshades replaced, and other adjustments made. The selection of a designer—or a client—should be handled with great care, as the relationship can last for many years. In a successful relationship, designer and client become part of each other's lives. Thad Hayes certainly has become a happy and productive part of our lives.

You will surely enjoy and appreciate the beauty and comfort you shall see in the pages of this glorious compendium of Thad Hayes's accomplishments.

Up in Thad Hayes's bi-level office on the eighth floor of the Bryant Park Studios at 80 West Fortieth Street in Manhattan, the world appears to be a particularly charmed place. Designed by architect Charles Alonzo Rich in 1901 for Abraham Archibald Anderson, a well-heeled portrait painter and philanthropist who studied art in Paris after the Civil War, the Beaux Arts–style building includes twenty-four double-height artists' spaces with monumental north-facing, copper-encased windows featuring unobstructed views of Bryant Park below, the west facade of Carrère and Hastings's 1911 New York Public Library, and the layers of towering skyscrapers that make up the midtown skyline from Forty-second Street north. Over the last century, the ten-story brick, limestone and terra-cotta landmark has been home and/or studio to an unimpeachable group of artists: among them painters Winslow Homer, Fernand Léger, and Florine Stettheimer; and photographers Irving Penn, Edward Steichen, and Bert Stern.

In the 1980s and '90s, Hayes's eighth-floor office was shared by designers Joseph Paul D'Urso, Robert Bray, and Michael Schaible (the latter two of Bray-Schaible Design), who, in the minimalist "high-tech" spirit of the late 1970s/early '80s, painted the duplex's richly ornamented architectural envelope glossy white, laid down charcoal-gray industrial carpeting, and installed two massive white laminated drafting tables on black metal bases that echo the original black iron circular staircase leading from the entry vestibule to the mezzanine above.

It was here in 1982 that Hayes, fresh out of Parsons School of Design, cut his teeth in interior design, spending some three years working directly with Robert Bray, who, in 1985, encouraged his young assistant to strike out on his own. Hayes did, opening his own one-man office in lower Manhattan, where he lived, worked, and ultimately flourished.

Though Hayes's Tribeca office was also a bi-level space, its funky downtown charm was no match for the period grandeur of the Bryant Park Studios. And in 2003, after D'Urso had moved on and Bray and Schaible had terminated their practice, Hayes returned to 80 West Fortieth Street, securing the lease on the eighth-floor space where he had first apprenticed as a designer. Rather than reclaim the space with a massive renovation scheme, Hayes left things pretty much alone. In fact, save for carving out a small conference-room-cum-library by erecting a white lacquered storage wall and a row of black metal bookshelves, Hayes changed very little in the luminous space he first entered in 1982.

"I'll never move," says Hayes, who is not only understandably smitten with the space, but also content with the fact that his office can never expand. Given the limitations of the 1,400-square-foot space, the maximum head count of Thad Hayes, Inc., is eight, including Hayes, two or three designers, an architect, and support staff. With more space, Hayes could take on more projects, but to do so he would need to assemble a larger staff, which would necessarily mean abdicating some measure of control over his work. And for Hayes, control is essential. "I don't delegate," he says. "I direct everything. I'm in every meeting with every client; I go to every job site. I go to the upholsterer. I know every pillow fabric … every detail." Such a hands-on approach means that Hayes necessarily limits his practice to five "substantial" projects at a time. By substantial, he means they range in budget from $500,000 to $5 million—"not including fees"—and in scale from a one-bedroom apartment to a 20,000-square-foot house. At the moment Hayes is at work on three apartments at 15 Central Park West, architect Robert A. M. Stern's much-ballyhooed new residential tower overlooking Central Park; a pair of oversize 1870 townhouses in Boston; and a 7,000-square-foot apartment for an

*(Opposite) Private sitting room, West Side Residence, New York, 1998.*

executive, his wife, and their two children in one of Park Avenue's grander buildings. (Hayes designed the couple's first Park Avenue apartment in 1994, as well as the interiors of their weekend house in Westchester County, New York, completed in 1996.)

If you were compiling a list of designers to interview for, say, a "classic six" on Park or Fifth avenues, or a summer house in the Hamptons or Connecticut, or a winter retreat in Aspen or Sun Valley, the logical names on a list that would make aesthetic sense would be, in addition to Hayes, Jeffrey Bilhuber, Mariette Himes Gomez, Victoria Hagan, and, perhaps, Sills and Huniford. "People who are doing cleaner, edited design work," according to Hayes, who adds, "If the work were a political candidate, it's not far left, and it's not far right … nothing is too radical."

*Rigorous* and *restrained* is how Hayes characterizes his work, though the word *reserved* also captures something essential about his approach to design. The same could be said of the designer's personality, which is calm, considered, and as even-keeled as his interiors.

In an interview with the breezy online magazine *New York Social Diary*, Hayes speculates on the source of his obsession with order and control. "I think it happens to kids when their environment is kind of shaken up," says Hayes. "My mother and father divorced when I was in second grade … having order is the one thing that you can control if the family environment is a little unstable. I attribute it to that, but it could be genetic … you know, my aunt is very organized."

According to Boston-based landscape architect Douglas Reed, Hayes's college roommate and, more recently, his client for the interior of a new 2,300-square-foot weekend house (designed by architect Maryann Thompson) on forty-two acres in Southeast Massachusetts, "Part of what drives the way Thad shapes

space is his unrelenting drive for order, which I think is very personal, having to do with his own search for serenity. In the end, it informs all his projects. Thad is able to create atmosphere with an economy of means. I see Thad having that incisive decision-making judgment about making sure that all things work to express a particular idea or character. And anything extraneous ends up falling by the wayside."

Time-honored clichés about "upscale" New York decorators notwithstanding, there is not a hint of the diva, the dandy, or the prima donna about Hayes. He may have charm—and southern charm at that—but he is not what you would call suave. In fact, in many ways Hayes is the antithesis of the archetypal elitist New York decorator. In lieu of John Lobb shoes, Charvet shirts, and Hermès ties, for example, he tends to turn up in Levi's and blazers, khakis and T-shirts. And rather than attempt to bully or intimidate his clients into acquiescing to his ideas, Hayes asks questions, listens to the answers, and then responds with a scheme based on a client's program, predilections, and personality.

"Thad is so *not* a diva," says Brooke Neidich, a philanthropist, art collector, and advocate of improved mental health services for children, who has worked with Hayes on some seven projects over the last twelve years— including a large, prewar apartment on the Upper East Side, a rambling Shingle Style house in Wainscott, a Victorian ski lodge in Telluride, and a penthouse pied-à-terre ("for weekends") at the edge of Greenwich Village. (At the moment, there is talk of a possible beach house in St. Barths.) "There's a youthfulness to Thad. He's smart, even cool. He never gets upset. And he's a great listener," says Neidich. Case in point: for the house in Wainscott, Neidich specified "blue and white … Swedish." And Hayes obliged. But to counter the potentially "too cute and precious" palette, according to Hayes, he introduced a hard-

edged antidote. "Thad was wonderful, really a gentleman," says Neidich, who also worked with architect Alan Wanzenberg on organizing the expansive one-hundred-year-old house and companion "barn" for the three Neidich children. (Hayes designed the new four-bedroom guesthouse.) "I love the way Thad thinks about scale and size. When we were doing the house in Wainscott, I said 'I want it to be all white and blue,' and the first thing that arrived was this huge black cabinet. It anchored the entire living room, and I thought, 'Oh, I get it.'"

The Wainscott living room, with the 1860 French ebonized cabinet front and center, turned up in 2005 on the cover of *Architectural Digest*, which aptly dubbed Hayes "the Jil Sander of interior design."

From the earliest years of his career, Hayes has been popular with the press. In fact, his first commission, a six-hundred-square-foot floor-through apartment for the late menswear designer Terry Wilke, appeared in the *New York Times* in 1987. The total budget for the apartment, quaint by today's standards, was $65,000. Hayes also designed a showroom for Wilke that landed on the cover of *Interior Design*. Not long after, a rustic lakeside cabin in New York State for Evelyn and Leonard Lauder turned up on the cover of *House & Garden*, as did, a year later, a two-bedroom apartment for a young doctor in the San Remo on Central Park West. Hayes is also familiar to readers of *Elle Décor*, *New York*, and *House Beautiful*.

Nowadays, however, Hayes's work is most frequently found in *Architectural Digest*, where he has been named one of the magazine's "Deans of Design," and is regularly counted among the "AD100," the magazine's biannual who's who in architecture and interior design. Asked to speculate on his popularity with the press, Hayes says, "I think half of it is because the work is clean, edited, and easy on the eye."

Though precise and unpretentious, Hayes's work is also luxurious—but not in terms of conventional opulence. He is not one for over-the-top gestures or ostentatious statements. Not a tinge of vulgarity interrupts the serene aesthetic. Instead, he tends to create rooms that are inviting, rooms that are designed to be actively occupied, rather than just passively viewed. At first glance Hayes's obsession with order can appear intimidating: looking through the glossy, perfectly organized stacks of laminated photographs that document each of his projects, you search in vain for signs of something—anything—amiss. "I'm there for every shoot," explains Hayes, who does not suffer loose ends or random clutter. In other words, in the world according to Hayes, not so much as a telephone cord is out of place. "People do actually live in these spaces," reassures Hayes. "But it's true, I do 'style' every shoot."

Aside from sublime order, among the things you first notice in Hayes's portfolio is the palette, which has become evermore subtle over the years. Though he

frequently consults with New York color expert Donald Kaufman, Hayes is not one for polychromatic panache. He prefers a more monochromatic palette that does not dramatically shift as you move from room to room. No sudden splash of crimson or chartreuse or cobalt interrupts the aesthetic flow. No eye-catching faux finishes or flourishes draw attention away from the carefully considered whole. Instead, Hayes tends to opt for a calm, inconspicuous palette of white and ivory, ecru and linen, as well as earth tones and natural greens and blues and browns. Think subtle and nuanced, versus dramatic and theatrical. "I used to say, 'Oh, we can do color,'" says Hayes. "But I don't really like color. I don't like wearing it—I can't imagine wearing bright colors—and I don't like living in it. I think it's problematic. I tend to be more subtle and monochromatic about it because I think it's a good way to go."

Looking through the portfolio of work that Hayes has completed over the last twenty-three years, it is telling that no two projects look alike. While other designers leave their indelible signature on every home, you are not likely to confuse one of Hayes's projects with another. Each is unique, carrying its own distinctive stamp. "Conceptually, the projects are all over the place; they're very diverse in their elements," says Hayes, and it is true that his range is wide. From Austin to the Adirondacks, from Baton Rouge to Bethesda, Hayes creates unique solutions to each of the environ-

ments he designs. Whether working with preexisting architecture or a new building, Hayes seems less intent on imposing a rigorous aesthetic and more intent on revealing one that corresponds to both the structure and the client he is working with. He avoids jarring juxtapositions, melodramtic maneuvering, and all gestures of ostentatious showmanship.

In fact, no single signature "look" emerges. Instead, signature qualities come to the fore. Comfort and accommodation, calmness and serenity are key elements of every Hayes interior. Nothing is overwrought or overdesigned. He meticulously avoids such purely decorative items as elaborate window treatments, fussy tassels and fringe, richly patterned brocades and intricate toiles. Nor is he, at the opposite end of the spectrum, a proponent of hard-edged minimalism. The key, according to Hayes, is "Knowing exactly when enough is enough."

"My house has a kind of repose, clarity, and restraint," says one client. "There's quite a lot of subtlety and richness going on. The other thing that distinguishes Thad's work is warmth. His palette of materials is very sensual. So even though the work is restrained, there's a warmth to it."

Among the icons of architecture that Hayes points to for perennial inspiration are the Rothko Chapel in Houston, a 1971 collaboration between architect Philip Johnson and painter Mark Rothko, Eero Saarinen's TWA terminal at John F. Kennedy International Airport in New York, and Louis Kahn's Salk Institute in La Jolla, California. In terms of contemporary architects, Hayes singles out Renzo Piano, the Genoa-based architect responsible for the Menil Collection in Houston, the Beyeler Foundation outside Basel, the renovation of the Morgan Library on Madison Avenue, and the new tower on West Forty-first Street for the *New York Times.*

Hayes also admits to being particularly susceptible to the allure of such popular midcentury modernists as Charles and Ray Eames, Albert Frey, Pierre Koenig, and Richard Neutra. He finds their work "essential" and "optimistic," and argues that every interior, no matter what the particular style or elements, should have "a bit of that spirit." Think spare but not Spartan, lean but not mean, precise but not precious. "Hayes is Mr. Clean … a traditionalist who takes the stuffing out of traditional decorating," wrote *Travel + Leisure,* reporting on Hayes's work at Twin Farms, the posh three-hundred-acre Vermont retreat that designer Jed Johnson famously worked on until his death in 1996.

When asked which contemporary designers he most admires, Hayes says, "I always look at Peter Marino's work and at Joe D'Urso's work, and I always look at John Pawson's work. I still love walking into the Calvin Klein store on Madison Avenue [designed by Pawson in 1995]." As for Hayes's heroes in the design pantheon, they too are familiar. Asked to name the historic houses he most reveres, Hayes lists such venerable temples of high modernism as Pierre Chareau's Maison de Verre in Paris, Adalberto Libera's Casa Malaparte in Capri, Philip Johnson's Glass House in New Canaan, Connecticut, and Mies van der Rohe's Farnsworth House in Illinois.

Now fifty-three, Hayes came of professional age in the late 1980s and early '90s, a period when such design legends as Mario Buatta, Denning & Fourcade,

Thierry Despont, Mark Hampton, and Parish-Hadley were at the top of their game, when conspicuous consumption and over-the-top opulence were as celebrated as a jewel-encrusted Christian Lacroix pouf. Whether influenced by the minimalism of early D'Urso and Bray-Schaible, or by the lingering sway of Neutra, et al., Hayes belongs to that next generation of designers who take a more contemporary approach to design; that is, he creates rooms that are airy and light, rooms in which the furniture has sufficient space to breathe, rooms that are informed by an inclusive attitude toward design, enthusiastically mixing furniture and elements from the eighteenth century to the twenty-first century, rather than myopically adhering to one stylistic tack. Hayes subscribes to the mix-but-not-match school of design. Rather than creating historically "correct" period rooms or thematic interiors, he opts for eclecticism, confidently employing elements that vary in style, period, and provenance. And more often than not he does so with relatively limited input from his clients.

Given the scale of the projects he undertakes, it is somewhat surprising that many of Hayes's clients bring with them very little in the way of furniture and furnishings. Though there are notable exceptions—the Neidich Apartment in New York, the Lauder House in Palm Beach—clients frequently turn up virtually empty-handed for a project. "People come with not a lot of furniture … art, maybe, but not furniture," says Hayes. "A lot of people who are moving start over. They just get rid of everything. So, usually, in terms of furniture, there aren't a lot of restrictions." On the other hand, it is not all that uncommon for one of Hayes's clients to turn up with a Steinway, an art collection, and a wardrobe. It is Hayes's hand and eye at work, assembling contemporary furniture and antiques and vintage pieces that give the projects their look, feel, and texture. Which is fine with Hayes. "The way I conceive of a

project … well, to just throw in random elements is risky," he says. "It's risky even when the vision is clear. You're never 100 percent sure that things are going to come together perfectly and beautifully."

Hayes aspires to continuity, the ability to move from room to room with aesthetic ease, no sudden shifts in stylistic gears. "You want it to be compatible in the next room, but not to 'match,'" says Hayes, who likes to maintain a sympathetic tone and palette of colors and materials throughout the rooms of a house or apartment, however varied the individual pieces of furniture.

"Frequently with furniture from the 1930s and '40s, it's hard to get the right scale for the way people are living," says Hayes, who solves the problem by custom designing 40 to 60 percent of the furniture in any given project—from sofas and chairs to tables and beds. "There are still things we like to shop for," says Hayes. "It gives a lot of texture to the projects. Plus, I like getting out and having the chance to find something." Toward that end, Hayes is familiar at such popular resources as Bernd Goeckler in Greenwich Village ("He's great because he has everything from the nineteenth century to the 1960s," says Hayes), Wyeth in SoHo, and Liz O'Brien on Fifth Avenue.

Typical of this approach is the two-bedroom apartment he designed in the 1930s San Remo building on Central Park West for a young anesthesiologist. Hayes installed a 1940s Jacques Adnet macassar ebony dining table, which he mixed with pieces by such twentieth-century masters as Otto Wagner, Gustav Stickley, Charles and Ray Eames, Jacques Quinet, and Gio Ponti. It is almost as if Hayes set out to include one element from each decade of the century, a kind of twentieth-century sampler. He also custom-designed a sofa, a built-in daybed, and a club chair for the living room and library, and, for the master bedroom, a four-poster bed, which he flanked with a pair of quirky ebony and bronze biomorphic lamps that rest on art deco bedside tables. It is a suitably eclectic context for his young client's growing collection of contemporary art by Ross Bleckner, Peter Halley, and Cindy Sherman, among others.

As for the elements Hayes uses to construct a room, he is surprisingly egalitarian. He is just as likely to use a $500 mulberry paper lantern by Isamu Noguchi for Akari as he is to use a Lalique sconce, as likely to use a $649 wire-and-laminate Charles and Ray Eames 1951 "surfboard" coffee table as a bronze Giacometti coffee table. Explains one client: "I think Thad is brilliant at finding something that is a curiosity, that is inexpensive. But then he'll tell you that the lamps … well, except for the Milton Avery in the living room, the lamps are the most expensive thing in the house."

For the better part of the last two decades, Hayes has shown a special affinity for midcentury French furniture. For the East End Avenue apartment of Ellen Kern, an art consultant with a lively personal collection of contemporary work, Hayes and his client traveled to Paris to assemble a collection of furniture and lighting that would create a rich backdrop for work by Eric Fischl, David Salle, Susan Rothenberg, Francesco

Clemente, Ross Bleckner, Peter Halley, and Lucian Freud. Looking to the 1930s, '40s, and early '50s for inspiration, Hayes and Kern assembled a collection of pieces by such high-profile designers as René Prou, Maurice Jallot, Jean Pascaud, Jules-Émile Leleu, Jean Royère, and Gilbert Poillerat. The result is a lively dialogue between the art and the interior, which is the antithesis of the traditional "white box" approach to displaying art. There is a quiet exuberance to the apartment, a kind of discreet delight in the accumulation of furniture and art that is personal and idiosyncratic, as opposed to anonymous and generic.

For a grand prewar apartment overlooking Central Park on Fifth Avenue, Hayes laid down three white silk and wool V'Soske carpets in the living room, den, and master bedroom for continuity. He then designed and bought furniture that makes the transition from room to room an almost seamless experience. In the living room, he designed a thirteen-foot white sofa, a pair of white upholstered club chairs, and a massive bronze and glass coffee table that supports a black metal Alexander Calder stabile. The client's modern art collection—with canvases by such well known artists as Mark Rothko, Milton Avery, Adolph Gottlieb, Ad Reinhardt, and Franz Kline—is given pride of visual place, the obvious visual highlight of the living room. A pair of George III armchairs, also upholstered in white, flank the sofa, as do a pair of glass and bronze floor lamps, which Hayes designed for Boyd Lighting, and a pair of ebonized side tables from the 1930s by Jean-Michel Frank. Nearby stand a Steinway and a small round Poillerat table with a Calder mobile above.

In the adjacent dining room, a nineteenth-century Russian chandelier hangs above a round George IV mahogany table. A large canvas by American Abstract Expressionist William Baziotes welcomes the room into

the twentieth century, as do the two painted-wood free-standing fluted columns by legendary Hollywood actor-turned-decorator William "Billy" Haines that support a pair of fanciful bronze Maison Charles luminaires from the 1960s. In the master bedroom, Hayes installed a 1940s walnut and bronze desk by "decorateur des millionaires"—according to the subtitle of a 1990 monograph—Paul Dupré-Lafon, and, in front of the fireplace, a pair of leather club chairs with a companion ottoman.

The clients also commissioned the designer to decorate the summer house they built on the beach in Watermill. As is his custom, Hayes took his cues from the architecture: in this instance, a taut, clean-lined modernist house that rises gently above the Long Island dunes. Open and airy, the interior of the house is spare, outfitted with all the appropriate and necessary elements, and not one extraneous item. In the dining area, for example, Hayes installed a round Warren Platner table from the 1960s, which he surrounded with Mies van der Rohe's iconic 1930 Brno chairs, slipcovered in white.

"Thad is an appealing collaborator for an architect," says one client. And it is true that Hayes is both sensitive and responsive to architecture. He has the ability to

*(Left) Entrance gallery, Palm Beach house, Palm Beach, Florida, 1998. (Opposite) Living room, Greenwich Village townhouse, New York, 2002.*

appropriately respond to any number of architectural periods or styles, without compromising his basic aesthetic stance. "Even when a more 'traditional' expression is requested," adds the client, "Thad has a way of assimilating that into his modern spatial understanding and convictions to make it new."

In Palm Beach, for example, longtime clients Leonard and Evelyn Lauder asked Hayes to update the grand neo-Georgian waterfront estate that served as a winter residence for Leonard's parents, Joseph and Estée Lauder, since 1964, when the senior Lauders bought the imposing 1938 house. Given the family's rich personal associations with the house, Hayes's task was to refurbish, restore, and redecorate it without altering its basic DNA. After three years of work, during which virtually every system and surface in the house was updated, the result is that nothing dramatic appears to have happened. Rather, the impression is that the grand house has been gently eased into the twenty-first century—not so much redecorated as revitalized. Hayes reused as much of the existing furniture as possible, working with the Lauders to inventory and edit decades' worth of accumulated pieces. Where required, he introduced late additions, such as a pair of chairs by Pierre Chareau for the living room, and a quartet of plaster sconces that Diego Giacometti cast for Jean-Michel Frank in the 1930s.

Hayes's degree of involvement in the architecture varies from project to project. For a new house in Southern Maryland, the home of an author and his family, he spent the better part of a year drawing moldings and casework. "We designed every detail, every piece of millwork," says Hayes, who spent a total of three years working on the 12,000-square-foot house. At the opposite end of the spectrum, Hayes made virtually no architectural emendations to a small Manhattan penthouse pied-à-terre with a large terrace. "Think designer showhouse and get us in," urged the impatient client, and Hayes rallied in a record three months with a pale blue and white palette, wall-to-wall sisal, two wall-mounted Florence Knoll cabinets, Eero Saarinen's 1957 pedestal table, and, at his client's request, a pair of Philippe Starck transparent acrylic 2002 "Louis Ghost" chairs for Kartell. In front of the fireplace, Hayes installed one of his signature tailored sofas and a pair of upholstered lounge chairs.

Things are good," says Hayes. "I've probably never been so calm and settled." The designer is referring not only his midtown Manhattan design practice, but also to his home life, which dramatically changed in January 2004, when he and his partner, restaurateur Adam Lippin, welcomed son Daniel Luke Lippin-Hayes into the fold. Hayes describes family life as "warm and fuzzy and all those things you expect." Adding, "I love it. There's something that's just so different from the Monday to Friday thing." As for fatherhood, Hayes says, "I never expected it would happen. I didn't think it was possible. It's one of the great things that's happened to me. It has allowed me to become less focused on myself."

In January 2005, Hayes, Lippin, and then-one-year-old Daniel moved from a two-bedroom apartment that occupied the parlor floor of a grand 1830 townhouse on West Sixteenth Street in Manhattan, to a vintage red brick "center hall colonial" in a polite, well-established, leafy suburb thirteen miles across the Hudson. The three-story, four-bedroom house proved to be a fitting repository for the furniture from the Manhattan apartment, even though the vast majority of it was custom-designed by Hayes for the West Sixteenth Street space.

In the dining room and living room, both of which face the street, the windows are bare. "I keep thinking maybe I should put something on them, but I'd rather not do window treatments," says Hayes, who likes the simplicity and openness of the unadorned double-hung windows.

To replace the custom-designed twelve-foot dining table he sold to a client, Hayes bought a Gustav Stickley Director's Table, which he surrounded with the six leather library chairs he had made for the West Sixteenth Street apartment. In the living room, a free-standing mahogany cabinet Hayes designed conceals a television, and, by the fireplace, is one of two one-armed sofas he had made for a room in a designer showhouse, sponsored by *Traditional Home* magazine, to benefit breast cancer research. A pair of Ward Bennett's classic I-beam side tables from the 1970s stands by a pair of upholstered armchairs.

There are two pieces of art in the house that made the move from Manhattan to the suburbs: a 1999 etching by Richard Serra, *Bo Diddley*, in the dining room; and in the living room, a 2001 landscape by April Gornik, *Light in Winter*, that reminds Hayes of the view from a weekend house he once owned in Sag Harbor. On the mantel in the living room is another piece of art, an abstract drawing, framed and mounted on a small easel. It is son Daniel's contribution to the décor.

In addition to his second-floor bedroom, Daniel's domain extends to the house's basement, now a dedicated playroom fitted out with cabinets and cubbies for toys and books and soccer balls, and a large L-shaped sofa for reading or cavorting during playdates.

Spare and open, uncrowded and uncluttered, the house is peaceful and serene, luminous and lean. "I love the idea of not having many possessions or attachments," says Hayes. "I think it's very freeing to get to the point where you say, 'This is just stuff.'"

"'Waste not want not,' 'Cleanliness is next to godliness' ... all those puritanical, American ideals," adds Hayes. "I think in many ways I feel more aligned to the Shakers and other sects in which good, orderly behavior leads to a good life."

# CENTRAL PARK VIEWS

New York, New York
2000

The clients for this project, a Japanese-American couple with two young children, had purchased a new apartment in a prestigious Fifth Avenue building with an impressive pedigree. Their former apartment had been traditional and, as Hayes describes it diplomatically, "while pleasant and tasteful, it was nonetheless boring." They were ready for a departure in terms of both the architecture and interior design, and invited Hayes and an architect to design a new home where studied simplicity and furnishings of impeccable quality would preserve their cultural heritage.

Thus it was that Hayes, collaborating with both an architect and the clients, embarked on a complex, three-year project he describes as akin to "tacking a course through the ocean." The concept was highly calculated, even for a designer: each choice of a particular piece of furniture and architecture informed the subsequent selections, alternating among traditional American-English design, twentieth-century modernism, and Asian elements. "If we purchased late-eighteenth-century chairs, the next purchase was usually a modern custom piece or a great twentieth-century antique item," Hayes recalls. "By organizing our thought process this way, we could easily make corrections and constantly improve the result."

After the apartment was gutted (poor workmanship and age made salvaging the original details impossible), white oak was used throughout for doors and door casings, cabinetwork, and the extra-wide-plank floors. The honey-colored wood establishes a solid, traditional feel as well as visual continuity within the new, orderly flow of spaces. Moreover, it provides desirable contrast with the deep walnut, mahogany, and bronze of the period tables and chairs. Hayes plastered the walls of the principal rooms in a soft gray, and the densely woven silk rugs throughout the apartment were dyed to match.

With this monochromatic palette in place, Hayes and his clients gradually assembled a collection of antique furniture ranging from George III and George IV armchairs and tables to pieces by Tiffany and the twentieth-century French designers Paul Dupré-Lafon and Gilbert Poillerat. "We bought amazing pieces with great provenance and quality, which was awe-inspiring for me," says Hayes, who also added meticulously crafted custom lighting and details such as a bronze grille with Chinese-inspired fretwork at the entry to the private, full-floor apartment.

Each room expresses a distinct personality within a neutral interior dominated by off-white fabrics and upholstery. In the dining room, for example, the opulent form of a nineteenth-century Russian chandelier reflects the organic lines of an abstract oil painting by William Baziotes—one of several, mostly Abstract Expressionist artworks in the clients' collection. In the master bedroom, indigo-blue walls and matching Chippendale armchairs contrast with the limestone-colored trim and plaster used throughout the apartment.

The master bath and dressing room are perhaps the most dramatic and Asian-inspired rooms in the apartment. Two dark granite pedestal sinks float in front of a large wall of glass separating the shower; opposite, a monumental tub with matching granite rim anchors a wall that evokes Japanese shoji screens. "The room feels simple: brutal, yet elegant and restrained," explains Hayes.

The successful relationships between traditional and modern, organic elements and Asian influences, Hayes continues, "reflects the clients' innate love and appreciation of beauty and simplicity above all."

*(Opposite and following pages) In the formal living room, an off-white palette showcases art by Mark Rothko, Alexander Calder, and Milton Avery, and a broad range of furniture, from traditional George III armchairs to a pair of Jean-Michel Frank side tables.*

(Above) On the walls of the powder room, textured stone resembling bamboo leaves simulates "a night view into a Japanese garden," says Hayes. (Opposite) A Russian neoclassical chandelier and English mahogany dining table and chairs create elegant focus within the simple dining room. In the background is William Baziotes's Moby Dick, 1955.

*(Above and following page) In the modern yet tailored master bedroom, color appears in the deep-blue walls and a pair of Venini cherry-red glass lamps. A custom bronze bed frame delineates the sleeping space. Chippendale armchairs upholstered in white leather flank a desk by Paul Dupré-Lafon, ca. 1935.*

*(Opposite) In the study, a Tiffany parasol lamp tops a rare George III mahogany writing desk. Ad Reinhardt's Abstract Painting, 1950, hangs behind. (Following pages) The cool, massive forms of carved dark granite in the master bath contrast with the warm wood of the dressing room beyond. Shoji-like glass panels at left conceal a spacious shower.*

# PENTHOUSE ON FIFTH AVENUE

New York, New York
1993

This project presented a unique problem: how to extend the Fifth Avenue home of a highly successful, socially prominent couple for whom privacy had become one of the greatest luxuries in life. By any standard the clients themselves are exceptional: both husband and wife are involved in the family business, a multinational enterprise, and spend a great deal of time supporting philanthropic causes and serving on the boards of major cultural institutions. "They get things done," says Hayes. "They work constantly and rarely take time off." The couple had lived in their apartment since 1970, but it had become increasingly public over the years, used for benefits, events, and large-scale entertaining. When the smaller penthouse apartment upstairs became available, they bought it, hoping to carve out a quiet, more private retreat.

"The ideas for the two spaces could not have been more different," explains Hayes. The original floor was traditional, with dark, wood-paneled walls, French antiques, and a museum-worthy collection of artwork. By contrast, the couple wanted the new addition to feel light, airy, and unfussy. "From the beginning the clients' dictum was: reduce the moldings, strip windows down to the rough metal, use few or no window treatments … a light, ethereal look," Hayes recalls.

The first challenge was how to connect the two spaces. Hayes initially envisioned a dramatic, sweeping staircase from the lower-floor entry to the penthouse, but such a gesture would have made the penthouse almost as public as the main floor. Instead, he and the clients opted for an elevator to minimize circulation between the two floors.

In the new space, Hayes created an open layout—encompassing a living area, a reception/dining area, a master bedroom, his-and-hers bathrooms, a study, and an eat-in kitchen—that segues directly to an outdoor wraparound terrace with views of Central Park. At the wife's request, Hayes added bleached oak floors and left all of the windows exposed except those in the master bedroom, thereby allowing natural light to flood the rooms. Walls are predominantly a creamy, off-white tint that creates an almost seamless visual field with the floors. "The architecture, walls, and floors are monochromatic, and therefore read simply as consistent 'non-color,'" Hayes explains. A well-edited selection of paintings and sculpture accents modern and custom-designed furniture.

The master bedroom was envisioned as the most protected space in the penthouse—a luxurious cocoon. Built-in, floor-to-ceiling bookshelves line the walls, and windows are covered with heavyweight silk drapes, lined to block out light and noise.

For the clients, the overall openness, light, and views from this private apartment renew the spirit and are an antidote to ambitious schedules. While a feeling of calm reigns inside, says Hayes, "you feel in touch with the city around you and a connection to the great, green park below."

*(Opposite) Exposed windows, a creamy palette, and bleached oak floors create a light-filled, airy private retreat one floor above the owners' existing apartment. In the living room, Picasso's* Seated Nude Man *(1971) hangs above the mantel.*

*(Above) A painting by Judy Ledgerwood, Pool (1989), anchors the light-dappled reception/dining area. (Opposite) The master bedroom is a secluded, luxurious room for resting and sleeping. Above the mantel is a landscape by Gustav Klimt, c. 1903.*

*(Opposite) Though quiet and protected, the master bedroom is also connected to the outdoors, with views and access to the wraparound terrace garden directly outside. Matisse's Henriette II (1927) occupies the deep windowsill. (Above) The terrace has sweeping views of Central Park and the grand apartment towers of the Upper West Side.*

# GREENWICH VILLAGE TOWNHOUSE

New York, New York
2002

What do designers do when presented the problem of designing for themselves? Hayes skirted the issue for the first twenty years of his professional life: the two second homes he designed for himself in the 1980s and '90s, one in upstate New York and one in Sag Harbor, on Long Island, were both "anti-design," he says. "Those two houses represented escapes for me. They weren't about the perfect piece of furniture or paint color." Rather, they embodied Hayes's search for a sense of place and were united by their "naïve, purely domestic American landscape," he explains. "They were more an exercise in self-exploration."

By 2002, however, six months after the events of 9/11, Hayes's life in New York had taken a distinct turn, and an 1838 townhouse in Greenwich Village that he called home was about to become a totally different project. "A number of significant things happened that year, one being that my partner and I decided that we wanted to have a child, which would require rethinking the whole living situation." After several months of searching, Hayes found a Georgian-style mansion just off lower Fifth Avenue, with high ceilings, perfectly proportioned rooms, and two working fireplaces. "The bones were perfect, the location was very nice—with a south-facing, bright living room—and it had space for a child to boot. It just felt like a great old family house."

Initiating the ambitious design process, however, was "painful, fearful, and exhilarating," as Hayes describes it. He sought advice from his mentor, the New York–based designer Robert Bray, who urged Hayes to keep his scheme simple and clear. "I was most concerned with having a home that looked liked a designer lived in it. That was the problem in a nutshell: I really did want to design this house, but I didn't want it to look designed," recalls Hayes.

He first worked on structural elements, duplicating the thick exterior walls, with their original raised panels and frames, as interior walls. The new walls initiated a rhythm and lent substance and elegant proportions to the spaces. Hayes also installed new floors, added bathrooms, and designed furniture for the space, combining it with antiques and found furniture. "By layering period styles, you force the viewer to make mental jumps, stylistically as well as chronologically, thus suggesting that design is perhaps a chance occurrence, an accidental collision of ideas and thoughts," he says of his approach.

He strictly limited the palette, materials, and fabrics to unify and connect the rooms: three fabrics and one type of rug are used throughout, and the restrained color scheme, devised with painting consultants Donald Kaufman and Tafy Dahl, is based on the three fabrics. Two American elm tree trunks provided the wood for the living-room table, the twelve-foot-long dining table, and the bed in the master bedroom. The bases for the pieces were made from black I-beams, Hayes's nod to the modernist architect Mies van der Rohe. The resulting rooms are neither modern nor traditional. Hayes describes them as having a quiet, elegant naturalness "that never looks overwrought, polished, or slick, but maintains a meditative quietness," a quality he finds in classic modern architecture as well as in Japanese architecture, which he studied in college and further grew to appreciate while spending time in Kyoto, Japan.

The Greenwich Village townhouse allowed Hayes to explore his personal and professional development without limitations, and represented a homecoming rather than an escape. "I wanted our house to embrace and fulfill all the romantic notions we have around the idea of 'home': the welcoming of friends, cooking, children's chatter, sitting around a hearth. That was really my expectation," he concludes.

*(Opposite) In the living room, Hayes contrasted industrial and romantic elements and created a deep-set paneled wall (right) that emphasizes the muscular architecture. A wool and leather sofa and a steel I-beam side table by Ward Bennett play off a landscape painting and a 1930s Lachenal buddha.*

(Above) Anchoring the living room is a large, custom-designed American elm and steel table and its centerpieces, two monumental antique Chinese scholars' rocks. The leather chair in the foreground, a Hayes design based on a 1940s library chair, and the Asian-inspired woven floor mats repeat in the dining room and bedroom, creating visual consistency throughout the house.

(Above) In the dining room, which receives little natural light, a warm, dark shade paradoxically opens up the space. "When the walls went dark, they fell away to shift the focus to the center of the room and the dining experience," Hayes says. An Isamu Noguchi paper lantern hangs moonlike above the American elm and steel dining table. (Opposite) Furnishings in the living room were edited to a precise expression of geometry and proportion. They include a 1950s antique brass and inlaid mother-of-pearl mirror and a custom mahogany storage cabinet with brass hardware.

# A COLLECTOR'S PIED-À-TERRE

New York, New York
1996

The client for this project was a single woman who had purchased an unassuming two-bedroom apartment as a pied-à-terre in the city so she could be close to her children and grandchildren, museums, and cultural events. She asked for an elegant, simple shell that would accommodate part of her collection of museum-quality artwork. The extremely focused collection, which she and her late husband had begun assembling in the 1950s, was divided into three disparate periods, consisting of Greek and Roman antiquities; minimalist and abstract works, mainly from the 1950s and '60s; and Old Master drawings and works on paper.

In addition to creating a space that would showcase and complement the client's artwork, a driving consideration in the project was her desire for a working office in one of the main rooms, where she could sit and write comfortably. "She wanted a beautiful space instead of being pushed into a corner of the kitchen or bedroom, which is so often the case," Hayes explained.

The assignment called for a complete renovation. Hayes began by enlarging and aligning doorways to provide framed views for the artwork, and replacing casings, baseboards, and trims. The entrance hallway was reconfigured into the apartment's main gallery space by removing three doorways that broke up the wall; Hayes redirected access to the bedrooms through a vestibule, which left the hallway walls free for displaying art. Hayes also designed a new kitchen and new lighting throughout. "The lighting had to be completely thought out so it could accommodate the art and antiquities," he explains.

Finally, Hayes created a handsome library and office in the dining room by adding floor-to-ceiling bookcases in dark American walnut, which include storage for files, printers, and a copier. The room's centerpiece is an oak library table from the aesthetic movement that serves equally well as a place to write and a dining table for guests.

Given the remarkable collection of art displayed in the apartment—including a Greek marble head on the fireplace mantel, flanked by a Boucher drawing and an Agnes Martin canvas—Hayes's challenge was to determine the best way to incorporate furniture into the overall scheme. To keep the focus on the art, most of the furniture, from the upholstered sofas in the living room to the beds and coffee tables, is extremely simple and monochromatic. Yet Hayes felt he needed "a way to bring some texture and life to the furniture that would prevent the apartment from looking too museum-like when completed." A solution was found in the client's burgeoning interest in furniture from the English aesthetic movement of the 1870s and 1880s, when architects and designers extolled the virtues of beautifully handcrafted furniture, often with sensuous lines and Japanese influences.

Hayes traveled to London with his client to purchase several pieces, including the library table and an ebonized wood cabinet by E. W. Godwin that helped balance the living room's quirky proportions. Throughout the apartment, Hayes says, "the overall effect is simple, yet the eye wanders from surface to wall to pedestal to vitrine, taking in all the wondrous art." Though the client's collection has been studied by scholars and exhibited by museums, Hayes maintains that "the success of the apartment, which is fairly modest in scale, is that it is first a home away from home, a place for the client to be with her grandchildren and family. In addition to that, the time she now spends at home, surrounded by her art, really is like a day at the museum."

*(Opposite) The living room balances the client's varied collection of art with aesthetic movement furniture, such as a rare ebonized wood display cabinet by E. W. Godwin (far right), ca. 1875.*

*(Previous pages, above, and opposite) Custom sofas and a pair of walnut coffee tables in minimal shapes keep the living room visually simple. A nineteenth-century African sculpture flanks a painting by Kenneth Noland, Fair (1960).*

(Opposite) A dark walnut bookcase creates a handsome office and library in the dining room. The English oak library table is a multipurpose centerpiece for writing and entertaining. (Above) A Jansen console in the entrance gallery displays a collection of 1960s Swedish stoneware and African and Native American sculpture. The armchair is by Scottish architect and designer George Walton, 1895.

# A STATELY MARYLAND RESIDENCE

Southern Maryland
2004

From its inception, this complex project, a new house on one of the last remaining large tracts of land near Washington, D.C., was about combining the sensibilities of past eras with several different period styles to create an interior that is gracious and somewhat grand, yet comfortable for family living. The clients, an author and his wife, a teacher, are consummate bibliophiles with a large collection of decorative objects from around the world. At the time their house was designed, they had two high school–age children preparing to leave the nest. Furthermore, the house had to be adaptable for entertaining large groups as well as for smaller dinners with friends.

In addition to these pragmatic considerations, the clients expressed a love of gardening and landscape, and admiration for the rambling houses of the 1920s and 1930s in the Main Line outside of Philadelphia, with their eclectic architectural styles. "I took this as a cue that a broad range of design periods should be considered," says Hayes, adding, "The key and difficulty is to combine this concept with contemporary living." Yet Hayes immediately felt drawn to the values and optimism embodied in these earlier houses. "There was an economy to their overall design that allowed the inhabitants to sense spaciousness and luxury without the emptiness and coarseness that can be present in residential design culture today," he explains.

Hayes spent the first year of this three-year project drawing architectural elevations and plans in collaboration with the architect, working with the firm on lighting and selecting the palette of materials. Hayes noted early on the wife's preference for certain soft colors and for rooms that were romantic but not too traditional or stodgy. The clients, he explains, "tend to be fairly serious and the interiors reflect that. They also reflect her desire for things that are inherently beautiful." As a result, the architectural materials represent a range of colors, from soft gold, beige, and off-white to pale green and pink, unified by creamy golden limestone flooring throughout the house. "The process for designing the interiors was organic," says Hayes. "We began with a floor plan and a single antique carpet for the living room, and everything else followed." He acquired two additional antique rugs with similar hues, installing them in the study and master bedroom; the three carpets unify these main rooms even though their specific furnishings vary in style and period.

Throughout the house, the pale yet warm flooring, wall paint and finishes, and upholstery temper the effect of more dramatic details such as period lamps and chandeliers, custom-designed tables and wall paneling, and found pieces. "We selected a variety of things ranging from late-1700s English dining chairs to a late-1950s Charles lamp from Paris," Hayes says. In the master bathroom, for example, pink stone covers the entire floor and walls. "A device that I often use, and I did in the case of the pink bathroom, was to formulate a simple, more rigid architectural vocabulary of detailing the wall panels, which balances the softer, more romantic pink stone."

Yet for Hayes, it is the "small considerations," not necessarily the architectural detailing or furniture, that make this house unique. From the master closet, for example, there is a beautiful view to the lower terrace and English-style gardens at the rear of the house. "In my own personal experience, what makes a home special are those wonderful views from a window out to a tree, or the constantly changing landscape and sky that suggest to me that homes and interiors are temporal regardless of the importance placed on them," Hayes concludes.

*The house's axis culminates in this formal seating area in the living room, where a nineteenth-century Italian gilt-wood mirror adds drama to the gracious interior.*

(Pages 52–53) The grand main entry hall begins a formal procession through the house, leading to the dining room through double doors and living room. Creamy limestone flooring unites a diverse mix of art and furniture, including a marble-topped, patinated iron table by Gilbert Poillerat, ca. 1947, and a late-nineteenth-century Japanese lacquer chest.

(Previous pages) The sitting room is designed for entertaining; seating options include comfortable custom sofas and chairs, an English 1940s art moderne armchair, and a pair of 1920s Moroccan ottomans with mother-of-pearl inlay. Here, as throughout the house, the color palette ranges from off-white to pale green and gold.

(Above) An antique Indian carpet selected for the living room combines solid tradition with soft, romantic colors and was the starting point for the interiors. On the wall, a pair of Japanese paper screens with trompe l'oeil detailing, ca. 1820, complement the antique Japanese cabinet in the entry hall beyond. (Opposite) The dining room includes a set of George III mahogany dining chairs in the style of eighteenth-century English cabinetmaker George Hepplewhite. A pair of chairs flanks the entry to an anteroom with a 1940s French parquetry cabinet by Jules Leleu.

(Previous pages) Chinoiserie wallpaper, with a bird and floral motif hand-painted on silver leaf, dominates the formal dining room. Complementary Fortuny fabric covers the George III chairs. A collection of the client's hand-painted, early-nineteenth-century Chinese "bobbin" figurines accents the table.

(Above) The long custom dining table, with three pedestals, comes apart to form three separate square tables that can be expanded for entertaining. (Opposite) The conservatory opens to the garden and features a custom table and a set of ca. 1925 Swedish painted art deco side chairs suitable for an informal lunch or tea.

*(Above) The kitchen opens to a breakfast area and family room, with a screened porch beyond. In the breakfast nook, 1930s French chairs surround an English aesthetic movement table. Lighting ranges from antique Holophane fixtures over the kitchen island to the ca. 1940 Finnish chandelier in the breakfast nook.*

(Opposite) In the master bath, architectural detailing on the stone wall panels balances the stone's rosy color and organic pattern. (Above) With its antique carpet, art deco period pieces, and casual layout, the master bedroom is reminiscent of Main Line Philadelphia homes of the 1930s. "There's an ease to it," Hayes says of the bedroom. "I wanted to make something that looked like it had evolved over time." The elegant, 1937 silk-upholstered daybed is by American designer Eugene Schoen, with a Brazilian rosewood base and lacquered legs. The rosewood writing table is French, ca. 1930.

*(Above) Furniture hugs the wall in the master bedroom, creating a feeling of openness. Less formal design elements include an unmatched pair of bedside tables and a carpet that does not precisely fit the room. Artwork is classic: a Renoir painting above the daybed and a Miró above the fireplace.*

# EAST END AVENUE RESIDENCE

New York, New York
1992

The owner of this East End Avenue apartment, a success-ful art dealer, contacted Hayes after seeing a magazine article on a prewar apartment he had designed on Central Park West. The client was passionate about art and had a large collection of modern paintings and photography that she wished to integrate into the design of her apart-ment—which was, as Hayes describes it, stark white and "basically empty" as the result of a recent divorce settle-ment. "In this spacious apartment in one of the finest East Side buildings in New York, my client was living with two beige sofas in her living room and a plain bed in her bed-room," he explains.

The client wanted a new image for herself and space for her constantly evolving art collection, but also a comfortable living space and a home for her grown chil-dren and grandchildren. "She wanted it to be obvious that a strong person with a clear vision and conviction could have an apartment with beautiful, almost feminine ele-ments that were not traditional or cute. She was a down-town person who happened to love her uptown apart-ment," says Hayes.

Rather than modifying the architecture, Hayes transformed the apartment by introducing color to the walls and furniture that is classically modern yet organ-ic, without the "hard-edged, Miesian, museum look" favored by many collectors, he explains. Working with color consultants, he created a customized, creamy, yel-low-green palette inspired by nature. "The client and I had a conversation about the deep, bright, rich-green color of moss that grows on the ground and on trees in the springtime," Hayes recalls. "I had just been looking at this, in fact, and thought the moss looked like a beautiful mohair fabric."

Early on, Hayes and his client devised a detailed furniture plan and traveled to France on a buying trip, exploring antique dealers and flea markets. Purchases from the trip include furnishings by Jean Royère, Maurice Jallot, René Prou, and Jean Pascoud. The modern feel and distinct details of a Royère armchair are particularly well suited to the client's modern artwork. Hayes balanced these detailed pieces by designing additional furnishings that provide a warm, earthy feel, such as the fireplace and mantel in the living room. He unified the earthiness and modern detailing with a custom-designed wood-and-bronze table and room divider.

During the course of the project, the client tran-sitioned into a career as an art consultant, which required quieter evenings working at home. Many years after its completion, the apartment still provides a flexible and comfortable space for living, entertaining, and working. "It still feels fresh," Hayes says, "and nothing has been replaced, not even rugs or curtains. The art on the walls is occasionaly changed to match the changing moods of the client. The rest stays the same."

*(Opposite) The bold, organic forms of a 1940s Jean Royère armchair and René Prou table express the client's desire for beautiful design that stands up to her collection of contemporary art.*

(Previous pages) Liberal color prevails in the living room, with a rich moss-green palette and blue satin Italian chairs from the 1950s. "It's not timid," says Hayes, who added other elements of 1950s design such as the coffee table by Gilbert Poillerat. On the wall is David Salle's We'll Shake the Bag.

(Above) At one end of the living room is a 1950s red lacquer bar by French designer Batistin Spade and an untitled work by Susan Rothenberg. The lamp is by Royère, with a whimsical custom shade. (Opposite) Hayes designed a round table to balance the proportions of the square dining room, adding chairs by French designer Jean Pascaud.

(Following pages) The master bedroom is unabashedly feminine, with warm, pink walls and a 1938 bed by Jules-Émile Leleu, reupholstered in persimmon velvet. Above it is a study by Eric Fischl.

## WEST SIDE MODERNISM

New York, New York
1998

Renovating an apartment on the Upper West Side of Manhattan for a young professional couple demanded the full range of Hayes's talents and resources, from reconfiguring the architecture to deftly balancing scale and color, to selecting new furnishings that were sophisticated yet had a touch of glamour. From an outdated, cramped, and overly ornamented space, Hayes wrested a modern, luxurious home that balances the clients' hectic Wall Street careers and passion for travel.

The couple had purchased a one-bedroom apartment adjacent to their own, just off Central Park West, and wanted to combine the two apartments into one. "They both are in the financial world and were looking for a clean, serene, and modern space to retreat to after stressful days at work," Hayes explains. "They like healthy living, good food, and plenty of exercise, and thought their living space should reflect that lifestyle."

Achieving this, however, required the architectural equivalent of a Hollywood makeover: Hayes stripped the newly purchased apartment down to its bones, removing paneling and moldings, ceiling beams, and some walls. Then, with a clean foundation, he set to work. He converted the living area of the newly acquired apartment into a master bedroom suite that opens to a sumptuous private sitting room and office for the wife. The sitting room lies squarely between the two apartments, wrapped in a skin of burnished rosewood that links the existing unit with the new one. Overscaled rosewood pocket doors in the bedroom can slide closed to create this tranquil sanctuary. The golden lighting and suede-upholstered niche with daybed make the sitting room dramatic yet equally suited to reclining or working in solitude. Here and elsewhere in the apartment, pocket doors and enlarged doorways balance the high ceilings

and relatively small rooms; in the living area, thick rosewood shelves establish strong horizontal lines.

"We needed closets and storage to function perfectly, and we had to make this place beautiful—not pretty, but more handsome, in a non–gender specific way," Hayes recalls. The female half of the duo is "amazingly chic," as Hayes describes her, and the couple enjoyed traveling to exotic locations. To complement the wide range of art and books they collected, Hayes aimed for strong lines, elegant curves, and a clear palette.

Floors were stained espresso brown, and walls were lacquered in creamy white to establish sharp but clean contrast. Rich texture and generous proportions prevail in the form of plush fabrics, suede and leather upholstery, and custom silk rugs, all in predominantly warm, golden tans. "The play of the silk velvets and rugs against the roughness of the suede creates variety and tension in the overall scheme," Hayes explains.

In the master bedroom, the cool silver-blue of the barrel-back chairs and silk bedcover play off the lacquered red bedside lamps that lighten the mood. "I've always loved the sensuous look of a fine silk bedcover, regardless of its wrinkling, which is the charm of its character," Hayes says. The barrel-back chair, with its long bullion fringe, was inspired by "a French 1940s chair I saw once upon a time," says Hayes, and is repeated in the living area and the husband's office. Hayes added a few pieces by the midcentury designers Edward Wormley and William Haines, the Hollywood actor-turned-brilliant decorator.

The resulting apartment is clean, cheerful, and modern. "It speaks to a clear state of mental and physical health that I think we all aspire to, and certainly my clients do," Hayes says.

*(Opposite) In the library/sitting room, thick rosewood shelves with lacquer supports emphasize horizontality. The contrasting silk bullion fringe on the 1940s-inspired, suede barrel-back chairs adds texture and whimsy.*

(Previous pages) In the living room, draperies hang from a continuous steel rod that visually connects dissimilar window heights. Plush fabrics and furniture from the 1940s and 1950s, such as a silk velvet sofa by Ed Wormley, create a sophisticated interior. The center table in faux tortoise, gold leaf, and black lacquer is a midcentury American design and recalls 1950s Asian motifs.

(Opposite) A freestanding lacquered wall separates the dining room from the study. A set of 1940s walnut and cane chairs by Ed Wormley surround a custom mahogany table. The chandelier is a 1960s French design. (Above) Midcentury decorative pieces add a touch of glamour to the guest room. The dresser by Tommi Parzinger and gilt plaster lamp are from the 1950s.

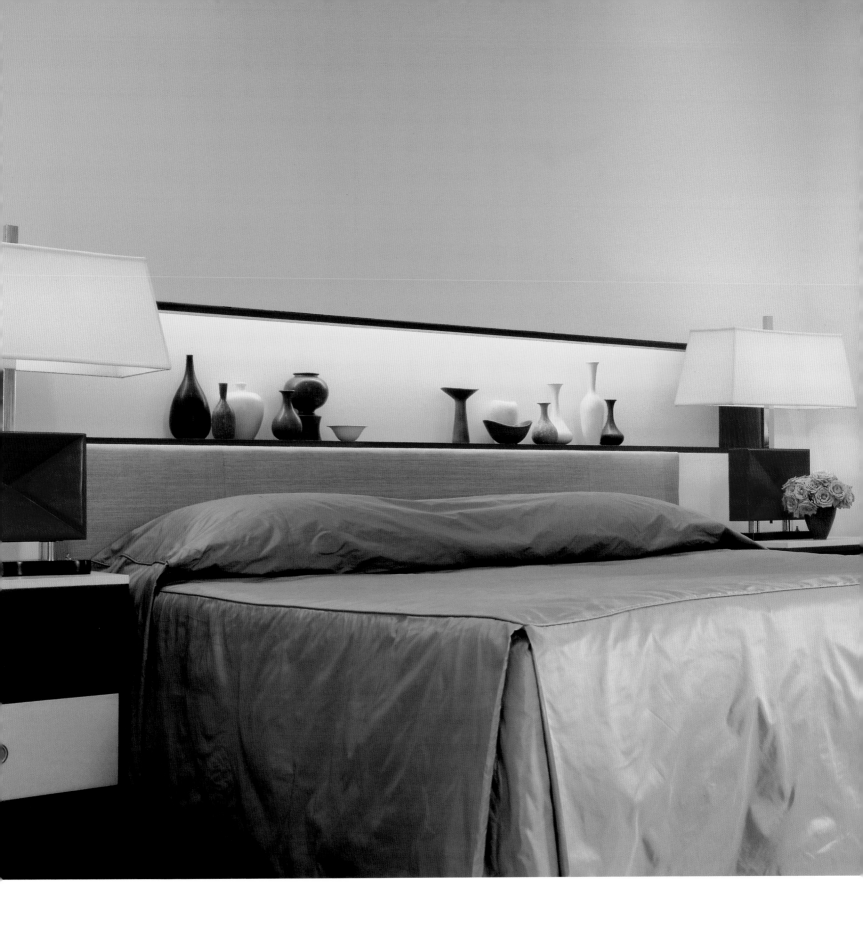

(Previous pages) Tall rosewood pocket doors in the master bedroom retract to reveal a private sitting room and office with a parchment and lacquer custom desk. The 1940s chairs are upholstered in silk velvet; the one at right is a design by Billy Haines.

(Above) Bright red and silver-blue accents in the master bedroom contrast with the creamy walls and linen rug. The red lacquer and copper bedside lamps are by Paul Lazlo, ca. 1945. The untitled ink and collage print is by Ellsworth Kelly.

# A CRAFTSMAN FAMILY HOME

Montclair, New Jersey
2004

This house, with its unabashed Arts and Crafts interior architecture and stucco-and-tile exterior, offered Hayes the opportunity to express his appreciation for Arts and Crafts design by retaining the original architecture and complementing it with period pieces. The four-bedroom house was built in 1908 in a charming town not far from Arts and Crafts and Craftsman schools, studios, and manufacturers, such as the Fulper Pottery Company. It presented a number of thoughtful period details, such as beautiful chestnut millwork, a grandly scaled receiving hall, and Grueby tiles in the dining room.

"I usually opt for allowing the architecture to speak and express itself but not rule or govern the choices made for the interiors," Hayes says of his approach. "For example, I would never design a period room for a client unless the client was a museum and wanted a period room designed. But this project was a little different. From the time I moved to New York in 1979, right out of school, I have always loved Arts and Crafts design." His goal was to temper the grand scale and linear quality of the wood staircase and beams to create a cohesive, livable environment for the owners, a couple with a toddler.

Coincidentally, the owners already had a substantial collection of Monterey furniture, manufactured in Los Angeles during the first half of the twentieth century, when the Mission revival style was popular. The sturdy wood pieces feature details and decorative painting reminiscent of Mexican furniture. Hayes used this collection as the basis of his interior scheme. "It definitely spoke to the interior of this house more than a lot of the other Northeast furniture companies of that period. The Monterey pieces looked unique and slightly askew compared to the typical things you see in the Northeast," Hayes recalls. He then selected Craftsman-style pieces, such as a large Gustav Stickley dining table and several large pots and vases, from the Bauer Pottery Company.

The main spaces radiate from the large, double-height entrance hall. Because this central space receives little natural light and features extensive chestnut millwork, Hayes chose a soft gray-brown shade for the walls to quiet the effect of the wood. Black-edged rugs in a synthetic material resembling sisal are used throughout the house to unify the rooms. The rugs are also a subtle reference to Japanese tatami mats, further linking the interior to the Arts and Crafts movement and its influences from Japanese and Chinese art and architecture.

The exterior of the house also influenced Hayes's treatment of the interior. With green tiles on the roof as well as decorative green tiles adorning the entrance, side, and pool portals, it "really looks like it belongs in Southern California more than in New Jersey," says Hayes. "The house has that old-world Hollywood flavor that I associate with the 1920s and 1930s. Because of that dichotomy, we were free to go beyond the notion of a Craftsman house and start to have fun mixing lots of different things together. Nothing was too precious." In keeping with this approach, Hayes added decorative chairs and a Hollywood table from the 1940s in the parlor, and covered an unused fountain in the solarium with a large-scaled ottoman.

The result, says Hayes, is a warm, muscular interior suitable both for the architecture and for the family that lives there. "They love the fact that their child can play in every room without the fear of precious and delicate things getting destroyed," he concludes.

*(Opposite) Hayes honored the original intention of a formal parlor in this Arts and Crafts house by painting the living room white and adding decorative furnishings reminiscent of Hollywood's golden era.*

(Previous pages) The living room and dining room radiate from a grand receiving hall with rich original chestnut millwork. The center table is from the client's collection of Mission revival–style Monterey furniture; the large etching is by Richard Serra. Tatami-inspired woven mats throughout the house unify the rooms.

(Opposite) In the dining room, a Gustav Stickley table, a Monterey console and chairs, and period details like a green Bauer pottery lamp and plates express the client's love of Arts and Crafts design. (Above) The fireplace is inlaid with Grueby tiles; the mantel displays Niloak Mission swirl pottery from the early twentieth century.

# DUPLEX ON PARK AVENUE

New York, New York
1993

The owners of this Park Avenue duplex—art deco enthusiasts, collectors of contemporary art, and active in environmental causes—wanted their home to reflect their modern sensibilities and principles. In particular, they wished to display an extensive collection of American landscape paintings and drawings, much of it large-scale and dramatic. "The primary focus for me was to respect the original, traditional nature of the apartment, but the clients' desire and interest in art and furniture pushed us into a new direction that was fresh," Hayes explains.

The space had not been altered for many years and required a total renovation. Hayes created a more gracious entrance gallery, adding new double doors on the main level, and completely re-designed the library, powder room, dining room, and master suite. He based the overall design on the idea of a quintessential 1940s art deco apartment in Manhattan—clean, streamlined, and elegant—then gradually expanded it to encompass a range of furniture and accessories from the 1920s through the 1960s. Since the husband is an executive in the cosmetics industry, Hayes says he sought to "instill a bite of glamour without it looking glitzy or over-the-top." Furthermore, materials had to be durable to withstand the wear and tear of an active family with two children.

The result of Hayes's renovation is a glowing, modern apartment whose beauty lies in the lushness and juxtaposition of materials and forms. Dark wood floors and dark brown doors add drama and sophistication, while upholstery and walls are light and airy. Mohair was chosen to make furnishings as rugged as they are attractive. In the library, Hayes designed a striking, V-grooved mantel in rosewood and mahogany that was inspired by a Frank Lloyd Wright detail. The built-in clock, Hayes explains, "was conceived as a whimsical nod to nineteenth-century mantel clocks, but in this case you can't move it. Time is present, not movable. We are forced to consider it and deal with it."

Likewise, in the dining room two enormous and provocative oil paintings flanked by luminous Italian sconces divert attention from an unconventional seating arrangement. Here, flexibility was crucial, because the clients often needed to seat as many as twenty-five dinner guests comfortably. Hayes collaborated with the wife to design a number of tables that can be easily adjusted, allowing for banquette seating on the perimeter, similar to a restaurant. "This was an unusual and challenging idea, but I embraced it, and I think the result is very successful, despite some interesting first reactions to the room."

Throughout the apartment, Hayes worked to marry the diverse scales of the space, furniture, and artwork. As he explains: "This was not a gut renovation, but it required careful analysis, precision, and an almost surgical removal and addition of details here and there to make the end product seamless and complete."

*(Opposite) The library/sitting room is a fresh take on traditional art deco. Landscapes by Chris Pfister, whose work the clients collect, hang above the custom mahogany fireplace surround with its built-in mantel clock.*

*(Previous pages) The entrance gallery view culminates in John Bowman's large-scale painting* The Middle Ages *(1994). Newly designed double doors incorporate art deco–like geometric detailing; both the doors and floors were stained dark to add a formal sophistication to the rooms.*

*(Above) A satin-upholstered custom daybed and sleek black Josef Hoffmann settee and table in the living room add glamour but respect the sophisticated, traditional nature of the apartment. (Opposite) Hayes designed five separate tables and banquette seating in the dining room to accommodate large-scale entertaining. Stephen Hannock's painting* Flooded Canyon: Yellowstone (Storm Approaching) *hangs above a banquette upholstered in quilted silk for durability.*

*(Following pages) Light-colored walls and luxurious fabrics, such as mohair on the custom sofa and chairs, contrast with the dark floors and doors. Robert Mapplethorpe's 1988* Apollo *hangs above a 1940s burlwood serving table. The stone, brass, and nickel coffee tables are custom.*

2 AS THE

E PEOPLE.

# TEXAS TUDOR REVIVAL

Austin, Texas
1998

The program for this Austin residence, a quirky 1927 Tudor Revival that had undergone multiple alterations and additions, was about balance: it required balancing the romantic desires of the wife and the modernist desires of the husband; accommodating the clients' fun-loving lifestyle and two young children; and unifying the house's sprawling yet somewhat dark spaces—including a large party room added in the 1950s—into a cohesive new identity.

"The husband and wife had slightly different ideas about what the house should be," Hayes explains. "She liked simple lines but tended toward more romantic notions of a house, visual warmth, comfort, and ease of operation. He had an architecture background and preferred clean, modern interiors but understood the restraints and context of this project." Despite the couple's aesthetic differences, Hayes's first visit to the house convinced him that their collaboration would be enjoyable—and memorable. Arriving early one morning for a walk-through with the clients, Hayes was warmly greeted at the front door by the former owner, who had dressed for the occasion in a backless silk taffeta gown and epitomized the house's history of elegant entertaining. "She was amazing! In a full-blown party dress, twirling around the house before breakfast was even served. I thought, Wow, this is Texas living at its best!"

Hayes first modified the structure by removing the large family room in the middle of the house, which was blocking much-needed light, and by adding doors and windows throughout the house to provide every room with multiple light exposures. Using French doors, Hayes further connected this new open interior with the house's luxurious grounds, consisting of several acres of land in the center of the city.

Inside, Hayes conceived a design direction that would work equally well for both husband and wife, while allowing their differences to remain intact. A monochromatic color scheme for the primary rooms, he felt, would neutralize any disparate elements. He provided depth by staining the oak floors brown-black; he then introduced a warm gray-taupe palette that appealed to both the romantic and modern sensibilities. The gray-taupe scheme and dark wood floor, Hayes felt, would also be visually pleasant and calming on extraordinarily hot summer days.

Throughout the house, Hayes combined mid-twentieth-century furnishings with his own designs, including the master bedroom bed and side tables. In the master bedroom, Hayes introduced color, a soft blue-green that feels serene and cool. The landscape wall panels by Piero Fornasetti were found later but, coincidentally, work perfectly with the color scheme. "So much of design is that way," Hayes says. "Finding art and rugs after decisions are made is as valid as doing it early on. It really just depends on timing and luck."

In the dining room, velvet-clad Samuel Marx chairs illustrate the designer's facility with luxury and minimalism. To the chairs and custom-designed dining table, Hayes added an eclectic array of objects, like Purcell fixtures from the late 1940s and a chain-link lamp in the living room with a uniquely Texan character.

The generally understated character of the main rooms stands in contrast to the wife's sumptuous private bath. With its pale walls, black-and-white marble floors, and porcelain tub, the bath is a glamorous yet modern retreat. Hayes's ability to weave both of these sensibilities together resulted in an "absolutely smooth" design process, he says. "That really is the secret to keeping couples engaged in the process and ultimately happy in the end."

*(Opposite) In response to the hot Texas climate, Hayes chose a taupe-gray color scheme and stained the oak floors dark to create a feeling of calm and coolness in the main living space, with its collection of eclectic furniture from the 1940s and 1950s.*

(Above) Hayes opened up the dark original interior of the 1927 Tudor Revival house but celebrated its quirky architecture, such as a Moorish arched entry hall. (Opposite) In an intimate living-room seating area, the sensuous lines of a custom chair complement the organic forms of a photograph by Imogen Cunningham.

(Previous pages) In the dining room, thick velvet curtains evoke the elegance of the 1920s and connect visually with the dark-stained floor. A rare set of ten velvet and lacquer chairs by American architect-designer Samuel Marx surrounds a custom walnut dining table.

(Opposite) A soothing blue-green palette prevails in the bedroom, where soft taffeta curtains and a quilted satin bedspread balance the modern lines of a custom bed. The iron and brass lamp, one of a pair, is French, ca. 1940.
(Above) Her master bath and dressing room is a glamorous private retreat. The unusual furnishings include a Lucite chair by Grosfield House, ca. 1930, and a pair of aluminum and glass lamps by Russel Wright, ca. 1940.

# PALM BEACH LEGACY

Palm Beach, Florida
1998

When Hayes was commissioned to restore and modernize this eclectic and grand house, one of Palm Beach's few oceanfront properties, it was already layered with history in the form of both family memories and an extensive collection of furniture assembled by the client's mother, "one of the great and glamorous style-makers" of the postwar era, as Hayes admiringly describes her. The house was built in 1938 and designed by Marion Sims Wyeth, a well-known society architect of the time, in a style that mixes colonial revival and Mediterranean elements. The client's mother had purchased the house in the mid-1960s, keeping some of the original owners' furnishings and gradually adding more over the years. When she passed the property on to her son and his wife, they asked Hayes, along with an architect and landscape designer, to bring this much-loved but dated family house into the twenty-first century.

The design team was dedicated to restoring the house to its original look and feel while updating it to reflect the clients' younger, more modern taste and lifestyle. "Part of the design solution was coming up with a concept that would embrace the history and tradition in the house since the '60s, as well as respect the original architecture," Hayes explains. The two-and-a-half-year project required replacing all the mechanical systems, meticulously refinishing all surfaces in the house, restoring many of its original fixtures, and editing almost seventy years of accumulated possessions.

In the bright kitchen, one of the family's favorite rooms, Hayes retained the solid 1930s and '40s feel by restoring major appliances, including the original glossy white-and-chrome range and wall-size refrigerator, and added new cabinets and countertops. Similarly, in the bathrooms, he refurbished the splendid original art deco sinks and fixtures, leaving exposed bulbs in the bathroom that proved to be a surprisingly modern detail. Cypress paneling in the library was also refinished to expose its original warmth.

To address the daunting mix of existing furniture, Hayes and his clients first completed an exhaustive walk-through of the house, discussing each piece and cataloging every possession with a color-coded tag. "This was not exactly a scientific method by any means," Hayes explains, "but we weighed things like intrinsic beauty, function, sentimental importance, and historical significance." Despite extensive alterations, Hayes maintained a connection to the family matriarch by keeping many of her furnishings and adding twentieth-century originals, as well as reproductions and custom-designed pieces.

Because the tropical climate would damage significant artwork, Hayes achieved a sense of artistry through a combination of custom paints, printed fabrics, and whimsical vintage wallpapers. In the dining room, for example, Hayes commissioned the original Chinese manufacturer to reproduce the 1930s trompe l'oeil wallpaper. Finally, because many family members would be using the house, Hayes designed all the bedrooms in the style of a luxurious hotel, with club chairs, writing desks, and plush beds.

The elegant exterior of the home remains a paean to the traditional Palm Beach community, yet its interior reflects the transition and optimism of a new generation. "The 'new' home feels fresh, light, and lively. Walking in, you're greeted by a light, modern palette that suggests a casual and easy ambiance; immediately, you sense the charm and humor of my two clients," Hayes explains.

*(Opposite) A sunny, light yellow paint modernizes the entry hall while retaining the 1930s spirit of the house. A pair of Chippendale chairs flanks a bronze console designed by Hayes; above it is an early-nineteenth-century Chippendale mirror.*

*(Above) The house, designed by Marion Sims Wyeth in 1938 in a courtyard plan with a neoclassical entrance facade, is an eclectic blend of colonial revival and Mediterranean elements. (Opposite) Woven grass floor mats, sheer curtains, and a well-edited selection of furnishings bring quiet elegance to the living room. The armchair is one of a pair by the French architect and designer Pierre Chareau. The pair of shell-motif sconces was a collaboration between Jean-Michel Frank and Diego Giacometti, ca. 1940; Hayes designed the thick, poured glass and bronze console, also one of a pair.*

*(Following pages) Hayes updated the formal living room with new pieces such as the upholstered stools and glass and bronze console, playing them against original pieces owned by the client's mother, including an American burled walnut secretary, ca. 1790.*

*(Previous pages and opposite) The formal dining room "was as much a preservation project as it was about injecting new life, in making it relevant for the people who were going to live here," says Hayes, who had the 1930s-era chinoiserie wallpaper painstakingly repainted by the original manufacturer. (Above) An intimate breakfast area in the dining room overlooks the ocean to the east.*

(Above and opposite) Designed for informal entertaining, the Florida Room was completely restored, down to the original paint colors, trompe l'oeil "pilasters" and trim, and coral floor. Hayes designed the rattan sofa, chairs, coffee table, and gaming table. A mirrored screen with rattan palm tree motif is American, ca. 1940.

(Following pages) Art deco details dominate in the family room, including a pair of open-back tub chairs from the 1933 Chicago World's Fair and selections from the owner's vintage travel poster collection.

(Pages 122–123) With its classical layout, the original swimming pool is surrounded by impeccably trimmed hedges—bougainvillea at left, a wall of ficus at the rear, and Australian pine at right.

*(Previous pages) Vintage wallpapers in the first-floor guest bathrooms preserve the house's original late-1930s character and reflect the clients' easygoing charm. The ladies' powder room, right, includes a found Lucite chair by Grosfield House, ca. 1935, and a French mirrored vanity.*

*(Opposite) A serene new breakfast room off the kitchen, overlooking the ocean, was the only addition to the original house. Hayes designed the dining chairs after simple wooden ones found in the house's attic. (Above) The kitchen, with its restored original range and wall-size refrigerator, is one of the family's favorite rooms and a repository of fond memories. Hayes added mid-1930s polished chrome and glass pendant lamps in keeping with the period appliances.*

(Opposite) Black-and-white family silhouettes in a second-floor anteroom complement the graphic lines of a Tommi Parzinger parchment leather cabinet and a pair of black wicker Wiener Werkstätte chairs by Josef Hoffmann. (Above) In a guest bathroom, whimsical touches include a floral-motif Venetian glass ceiling fixture, a refurbished art deco sink, and vintage wallpaper.

(Following pages) Guest bedrooms reflect the client's desire for the luxurious comfort of a good hotel room. Botanical-print draperies are paired with art deco–inspired, custom upholstered chairs. The green lacquer desk and chair and the burled maple dresser are 1940s French.

(Pages 132–133) From the outdoor terrace, residents and guests enjoy a spectacular ocean view across the front lawn. The ensemble of pink-hued furniture includes some of the original owners' shell-and-seahorse-motif chairs.

# PIERRE HOTEL APARTMENT

New York, New York
2001

The owners of this apartment in the Pierre Hotel asked Hayes to design a custom interior that would complement the clean, classic lines of the interior architecture by Alan Wanzenberg, with its combination of light bleached and dark Wenge wood. The Pierre is a renowned hotel and residential building on Fifth Avenue, across from Central Park, and is considered one of the best addresses in New York City. To Hayes's surprise, the clients wanted everything customized: all lighting, lamps, sconces, upholstery, rugs, and tables. "This was a challenging and very creative endeavor from the outset," recalls Hayes, who typically searches for a few special found pieces to give spaces texture and history, and to blur distinctions between periods. He recalls wondering, "Would it be possible for me to successfully design every element in the apartment and still maintain the layering and occasional quirks that my work has depended upon?"

Since the hotel provides all meals, the residence lacks a proper kitchen; and since it is a pied-à-terre, a large, formal dining room was unnecessary. The living space was already divided into two identical spaces of the same proportion, so Hayes created two matching living areas, which he referenced to the grand Victorian parlor and sitting rooms of the late 1800s. Because he was designing for two men, Hayes conceived an interior based on refined yet masculine materials such as bronze, leather, and stone. He designed a round, smoked-glass table that can be used for dining or simply as a center table. Dining chairs can be pulled up to the round table or used in the living spaces. In lieu of coffee tables, he designed large split-level tables of honed stone that are a suitable height for resting drinks and for displaying books and objects below.

The rest of the apartment contains a study, a large walk-in closet and dressing room, and a master bedroom. Hayes expanded on the combination of layered textures and height variations as a means of unifying the overall layout. In the master bedroom, for example, an upholstered wall grounds the bed and gives context to a simple wood headboard. To accommodate wall speakers below the windowsills, Hayes designed double-layer curtains throughout the apartment, consisting of a floor-length layer of sheer fabric paired with a short velvet top curtain. This functional requirement, Hayes explains, led to an emotional association. "The window treatments near the window are sheer and function symbolically almost as a feminine undergarment revealed behind the heavy, masculine, velvet 'Victorian' top curtain. This is intended to titillate and question the use of a window treatment altogether," explains Hayes, who prefers bare windows in his own house.

Throughout the residence, warm, monochromatic colors, 1970s-inspired chairs, deep sofas, and Wenge wood lend a sense of permanence to the hotel environment. "The irony is that at first glance the apartment looks like it could have been some amazing VIP room in an airport during the 1970s. I love this sense of permanence mixed with a more temporal attitude that airports and hotels have," Hayes says. Ultimately, it is this dichotomy between visual substance and temporal space that gives the project tension and interest, the layering and texture that characterizes all of Hayes's work.

*(Opposite) Hayes designed nearly every element in this refined, masculine apartment. In the entry, multiple layers and textures include warm silk walls, Wenge wood trim, and a suspended console below a custom mirror.*

(Previous pages) Leather club chairs, Wenge wood sofas, and bronze tables furnish twin sides of the monochromatic living room. Built-in shelves display vases by Danish artist Axel Salto and a work from the clients' collection of paintings by Mark Tansey; another Tansey hangs above the sofa.

(Opposite) The facing corner displays a painting and sculpture by Max Ernst, as well as a Louise Bourgeois sculpture on the Andes honed-granite tabletop. (Above) In the bedroom, a custom headboard with suspended night tables was inspired by classic 1950s motel rooms. Wenge wood, printed pony skin, and leather upholstery add a sense of luxury.

# MEADOW HOUSE

Southeastern Massachusetts
2005

Hayes was asked by a renowned landscape architect and his partner to design the interior for their weekend house in southeastern Massachusetts, sited on forty-two acres of meadows, wetlands, and low-lying woods, with a tidal river running through the property. The project was emotionally resonant for Hayes: the landscape was reminiscent of southern Louisiana, where he was born and spent his formative years with his client, who had been a college roommate and remained a close friend. Under such circumstances, Hayes normally would have declined the commission—assisting family and friends, he explains, is often "a sure way to destroy relationships." In this case, however, the deep personal connections and the client's "impeccable design sense" won Hayes over, he says. "I knew in my heart that this could be a unique and special opportunity to work with some amazingly talented people."

The client, the architect, and Hayes were further united by their training and interest in landscape architecture; for all three, the site with its natural vistas dictated the approach and design. "It was just assumed that anything that distracted from the site would be inappropriate, distasteful, even vulgar," explains Hayes. "The house, interiors, and landscape had to be quiet, elegant, sensible, and, most important, possess an economy to the total design." The single-level house has high ceilings and a long, narrow plan emphasizing horizontality, with an all-glass facade that affords stunning views of the meadows and river.

The client planned to plant sycamore trees in the large, flat meadow surrounding the house. In response to images of sycamore bark that the client sent him, Hayes conceived an interior palette based on a minimal number of warm, earthy tones: beiges, grays, and browns. He used two very American woods, walnut and white oak, for much of the custom-designed furniture and floors.

In the living room, an elongated, low-slung sofa and curvilinear chairs positioned over an off-white rug anchor one end. On the opposite wall Hayes constructed a shelf to elevate a stunning antique Japanese screen that the client purchased during the project. The screen, with delicate images of hawks painted on each panel, both delineates the dining area and links the inside to the outside, where actual hawks are often spotted diving through the air and fishing in the river. To the main seating arrangements Hayes added a limited number of unique custom pieces, such as a rectilinear oak side table and a glass lamp, hand-blown in a perfect sphere. "A lot of the furniture was custom-designed and is simple and basic, with craftsmanlike detailing and strong, elegant forms that are refined," says Hayes.

In the kitchen, the pantry, ovens, and all storage spaces are located in a thick wall that runs the length of the interior and acts as an axis dividing the living room and bedrooms from the kitchen. To provide ample workspace, the designers installed a thirty-foot stainless steel counter along one wall, overlooking the meadow. In the master bedroom, Hayes designed a simple metal bed frame and headboard and wall-hung walnut side tables. The two guest bedrooms are mirror images of this room, emphasizing openness and a lack of interior hierarchy. "The house feels warm and spare, but with all the necessary things one needs for a weekend or summer vacation," notes Hayes. "We even included a TV and music system, but usually the owners are reading on the deck, cooking, working in the garden, or just staring out across the meadow toward the river, listening to the birds and enjoying the gentle breeze."

*(Opposite) An Edo period Japanese screen focuses attention in the dining area, tying the house to the surrounding landscape of meadows and river. The granite-top table designed by Joseph D'Urso can be moved on its casters for window-side dining.*

*(pp. 142–143) In the main living space, furniture was upholstered in neutral shades inspired by the creamy tans, beiges, and whites of sycamore tree bark. Custom pieces include a Hayes-designed white oak console and sofa-back table near the window.*

*(Previous pages) A pair of 1960s Ward Bennett club chairs and a 1950s Norwegian rosewood coffee table form a clean, modern seating area in the living space. Behind the sofa is a pair of T. H. Robsjohn-Gibbings lamps from the 1950s with solid marble and bronze mounts.*

*(Above and opposite) A democratic approach to the use of art, furniture, and materials prevails throughout the house. The master bedroom and guest bedrooms feature identical steel bed frames and custom-designed, hanging bedside tables. In the master bedroom, above, Monique Prieto's 2002 painting* Day and Night *hangs above a chair by Hans Wegner. The guest bedroom chair is by Harry Bertoia; on the wall is Sol Lewitt's gouache-on-paper* Irregular Form.

# TRIBECA PENTHOUSE

New York, New York
2002

This duplex penthouse in downtown Manhattan, below Canal Street, was added to a former industrial space that had been converted to a residential building prior to the time Hayes's clients purchased it. The clients were a married couple expecting their first child and relocating from Greenwich, Connecticut, and Hayes envisioned their penthouse as "the perfect downtown New York family home." The space was modern, open, and loftlike, with several features that Hayes found exciting, including high ceilings and a large terrace. But the project also presented numerous challenges. Most dramatic was a structure perched on the roof adjacent to the apartment that had once housed the building's wooden water tank, one of the ubiquitous conical towers that give Manhattan its signature skyline. "When the wood tank was removed, what remained was a handsome brick structure just begging for some type of use," Hayes explains.

Despite being newly renovated, the building also had numerous irregularities in its facade and interior architecture, including sporadically located windows that ranged from unusually tall to small. "Our solution was to make a folding screen that would mask the blank walls and conceal odd sill heights, while maintaining a visual decorative element that related well to the furniture in front of it," says Hayes. Pale yellow chintz curtains hang from a track and diffuse soft light throughout selected rooms, while panels in the screens allow the clients to open the windows. To further develop a cohesive shell, Hayes selected a single, neutral-colored paint for the walls and upholstered the furniture in a warm palette of extremely durable fabrics. The hardwood floors were stained a dark shade, accentuating the pale limestone used for mantels and a long shelf in the living room.

In the challenging double-height brick structure that formerly housed the water tank, Hayes carved out a striking multifunctional room that functions as an office by day, family room and casual entertaining space in the evening, and children's play area at other times. Hayes calls this simple, industrial, almost leftover space "the pièce de résistance of the entire project." The walls soar up to the roofline, culminating in a skylight that bathes the entire room in natural light. The sunken living area is lined with banquette seating, with a shelf behind to conceal mechanical systems and support reading lights. The television, media equipment, fax, printer, and toy storage are concealed on either side of the stairs. To accommodate the clients' request for book storage space, Hayes designed an open steel-and-glass catwalk above the room, with industrial steel bookshelves hung on the painted brick walls. "I was drawn to the New York high-tech minimalist designers when I moved to the city directly out of college in the late 1970s," recalls Hayes, "and I felt that the inspiration for the design of this structure should come from that period."

On the second floor of the penthouse are the childrens' rooms, a guest room, and the master bedroom suite with a private terrace. Hayes characterizes the apartment as "extremely functional, durable, and very chic"— a classic example of the downtown loft redesigned for family living.

*(Opposite) A sculptural table by Edward Wormley occupies the entry hall. The hardwood floors were stained dark throughout to contrast with the neutral walls and pale limestone fireplaces.*

*(Opposite) A warm palette and sheer curtains enhance the living room's airy ambiance. The custom rug was inspired by autumn leaves in a dappled pool. The collection of American furniture from the 1940s and 1950s includes a Tommi Parzinger sideboard and coffee table. (Above) Fireplaces in the loft are uniformly designed in Indiana limestone, a common New York City building material. The chair is a 1950s Edward Wormley design for Dunbar.*

(Previous pages) Hayes reclaimed a roof structure to create a multipurpose family room/library with a steel staircase and steel-and-glass catwalk inspired by industrial buildings. The soaring ceiling culminates in a skylight.

(Above) In the main powder room, a white marble sink and checkerboard tiles evoke classic prewar New York interiors. Elegant details include lacquered walls and an Italian silver leaf and wood mirror from the 1930s. (Opposite) Hayes designed a tall headboard in the guest bedroom to resolve the unusually high window heights. The 1950s club chair is by T. H. Robsjohn-Gibbings, reupholstered in velvet.

(Following pages) A custom bronze bed frame forms a cube within the room. The abstract bronze table is by Philip and Kelvin Laverne, c. 1958.

# LOUISIANA HOUSE

Baton Rouge, Louisiana
2000

More than twenty years after Hayes left Louisiana to forge a career in New York, an out-of-the-blue phone call from a college acquaintance brought his life and work full circle. The acquaintance, a retired professional man who practices and teaches yoga, presented Hayes with what the designer recognized as "a once-in-a-lifetime" opportunity to work on a house he had just purchased in their hometown of Baton Rouge. But this was not just any house: it was one designed in the 1960s by the venerated Louisiana architect A. Hays Town, who interpreted Southern architectural traditions, from antebellum homes to townhouses in the French Quarter of New Orleans, to colonial revival design elements such as Spanish-style courtyards and patios.

Hayes had admired Town's work from an early age and, perhaps understandably, his reaction was mixed. "On one hand, I felt the opportunity to work on a house that Mr. Town had designed would be exciting and a privilege," Hayes explains. "The flip side was that I had never 'gone home' to do any type of project, and I felt a certain pressure to perform and prove myself as a designer." Hayes was quickly won over by the client's unassuming, gentle manner and by the signature elements of the Hays Town house, which included beautiful slabs of stone in the entry hall, high ceilings, and golden cypress wood paneling in the living room extending to trim and millwork throughout. "The materials—simple, elegant, timeless—are what really spoke to me when we began this project," says Hayes.

The client wanted a quiet, simple interior, a modern take on a respectable, gentile Southern home. As well as practicing yoga, the client entertains friends and hosts occasional fund-raising events for organizations in town. "We wanted the home to embrace openness and quietness, which is necessary for anyone on a spiritual path like yoga, yet the conservative context required some sensitivity," Hayes recalls. In short, the project was a balancing act, with Hayes attempting to achieve an equipoise between traditional and modern, an interior that was psychologically warm yet literally cool.

Because the summer climate is hot and humid, with temperatures often reaching into the nineties, Hayes kept the overall palette clean and light, adding subtle color to the wall paint to absorb bright glare. The wood floors were stained dark, which psychologically feels cool; sea grass carpets and linen rugs further temper the effects of summer heat. Natural linen, in fact, is predominant throughout the house in the form of upholstery, draperies, and bed coverings, and as an inspiration for the wall color.

Hayes designed most of the upholstery, then searched for found pieces, antiques, and antique lighting that appeared modern but at the same time had a handcrafted quality. Nearly every room in the house holds a piece by the twentieth-century American furniture designer Edward Wormley, whom Hayes admires for his skill at reinterpreting older forms into a clean vocabulary that bridges old and new design. As an example, Hayes cites the suite of Wormley chairs in the dining room, which, although mass-produced, are based on imperial Chinese chairs that are hundreds of years old. "This idea was the essence of my design for this home," he says. So while respecting the house's formal symmetry and traditional finishes, Hayes peppered each room with unexpected touches, such as whimsical 1950s light fixtures and a midcentury modern desk in the study, whose planar surfaces would be perfectly at home in a Southern California Case Study house of the 1950s.

Hayes remarks that since he completed the project the focus of the house has moved outdoors, to the gardens, which were conceived as exterior rooms with lush plantings and water, surrounded by the scents of flowering shrubs. Hayes describes the experience as transcendent. "My client admits that it is a difficult place to leave, and why should he? He can now practice his yoga and meditation both inside and out in total privacy, in an environment that supports and embraces his spiritual path."

*(Opposite) The study combines traditional masculine elements, such as a burgundy palette and leather armchairs, with a sea grass rug and linen-colored walls. The 1950s fish-scale chandelier adds an unexpected whimsical note.*

(Previous pages) In the living room, custom linen sofas and a matching linen rug establish visual unity and complement restored cypress paneling in the traditional Southern interior. As contrast, the 1940s coffee table, by Paul Frankl, has a lacquered base and a cork top with irregular sloping edges; the table lamps are also of varying heights.

(Opposite and above) The house contains multiple pieces by American mid-twentieth-century designer Edward Wormley, who "blurs the difference between traditional and modern," says Hayes. In the dining room, a suite of Wormley chairs in walnut, rosewood, and ebony are a modern take on antique Chinese chairs. The unusual cabinet with convex glass panels and shell pulls is by the eclectic American interior designer William Pahlmann. Designed in 1955, it resembles a wall of television screens and is a conversation piece in the otherwise traditional dining room.

*(Above) One end of the living room and the adjacent back entry hall display the client's collection of art and bronze. The black lacquer and mahogany console in the hall is by Paul Frankl. Black-and-white photographs on either side of the double doors capture views of Southern oak trees and palmetto branches. (Opposite) In the guest bedroom, a stone-blue palette, linen drapes, and sea grass area rug project coolness and serenity. Black accents include an ebonized side chair by Russel Wright from the 1940s and a pair of nightstands by T. H. Robsjohn-Gibbings, ca. 1950.*

# DESIGNER SHOWHOUSE

New York, New York
2000

Invited to participate in the Built for Women Showhouse for *Traditional Home* magazine, Hayes selected his long-time client Evelyn Lauder as the inspiration behind a room for an accomplished female client who has influenced society in a positive way. Lauder, the vice president of Estée Lauder as well as a widely exhibited photographer, an active philanthropist, and founder of the Breast Cancer Research Foundation, more than fit this ideal client description. Appropriately, ticket proceeds from the showhouse were being donated to breast cancer research.

Envisioning a calm retreat for socializing or quiet creative pursuits, Hayes created a modern, serene space whose minimal detail and warm, monochromatic palette were punctuated by boldly scaled furnishings and artwork. "I imagined that the room would be a place she could retire to for relaxation and meditation, away from her home and office. I could see her making calls for fund-raising events, editing photographs, or having a quiet meeting with a business associate, or tea with a friend," Hayes says.

The showhouse consisted of a sitting room and adjoining small studio within a traditional shell. "I wanted the first room to feel inviting, like a living room, but very modern and controlled. This would be a great place for two or three people to converse around the hearth," Hayes explains. Here, in front of the fireplace, twin rectilinear sofas custom-designed by Hayes divided a nearly perfect-ly square space, facing each other across an elliptical coffee table by Charles and Ray Eames. An overscaled spherical Isamu Noguchi lantern floated above the table, providing a dramatic counterpoint to the room's linear geometry. Artwork and accessories in organic shapes added an element of luxury: 1950s Swedish vases in rich black decorated the mantel, a Noguchi stone sculpture sat on the coffee table, and a Willem de Kooning ink-on-paper drawing was displayed on an easel lamp.

The studio's overall color palette was a soft gray-green; wall paint was custom-formulated to match, and Hayes selected a matching sisal rug. "I'm a big fan of gray, black, and white, but felt that Mrs. Lauder required a hint of color. By keeping the coloration and value the same, the overall effect is still, quiet, elegant, and modern," Hayes says.

In the adjoining studio, a smaller spherical Noguchi lantern hung above a large square worktable designed by Hayes, where Mrs. Lauder could review photographs and projects, make phone calls, and hold meetings. Though the project was not a permanent showcase, Hayes's client instantly felt at home. "I knew the room was a success by Mrs. Lauder's expression at the opening-night gala," Hayes recalls. "She proudly showed it to people visiting the house all evening. She even perched on the sofa in a playful manner to demonstrate how she looked in the room."

*(Opposite) Minimal but elegant furnishings contrast with the traditional architecture in this serene retreat for a busy professional woman. Hayes carefully controlled the soft gray palette, keeping color values equal for a quiet, modern effect.*

(Previous pages) Hayes began the design with the "simple gesture of two sofas," with deep cushions upholstered in a luxurious silk/mohair blend. Furnishings like the Eames "Ellipse" coffee table, topped with a sculpture by Isamu Noguchi, are elegant yet unpretentious.

(Opposite) Under a soaring ceiling, linear furniture keeps low to the ground and an overscaled Noguchi paper lantern becomes a dramatic counterpoint. A landscape painting by Alex Katz anchors the rear wall. (Above) The clean lines of a nineteenth-century decorative Chinese box and 1950s Swedish vases complement two rectilinear custom oak consoles with lacquered tops.

# SOUTHAMPTON BEACH HOUSE

Southampton, New York
2005

Despite the enduring presence of lovely, understated homes in the Hamptons, the so-called McMansions, with their ostentatious architecture and over-the-top décor, often dominate the public's perception of this charming and once-quiet string of beach communities on Long Island. When the clients for this oceanfront property in Southampton approached Hayes to do the interior architecture, interiors, and landscape design, he knew the project would not be, in his words, "your typical Hamptons beach house." Hayes had worked on the clients' New York apartment in the early 1980s as an assistant at Bray-Schaible Design and knew the couple required "pared-down simplicity, elegance, and a high degree of craftsmanship," Hayes explains.

The two-story, shingle-style house is surrounded by the ocean on one side and acres of cornfields on the other. The house's main living area is elevated a full floor above the garden and oriented to take advantage of the sweeping views. Both husband and wife spoke of the colors of the water, sky, and general atmosphere as a basis for the aesthetic, and responded to simple, somewhat muscular forms. "They had a very strong point of view about the kind of emotion that the combination of materials and colors would evoke," says Hayes. "In early meetings, the wife talked about walking on the beach when the weather was overcast, moody, and perhaps brooding. I had the sense that these people didn't need perky colors to make them feel any particular way."

Hayes first selected fabrics and rugs in a similar, muted taupe and warm gray palette. He custom-designed much of the furniture in simple, boxy shapes designed to draw as little attention as possible to the furniture itself. Then he enlisted the help of color consultants to develop a direction for the wood paneling, millwork, and floors, along with paint colors for the entire interior and exterior of the house. The wood was steel-brushed, bleached, and carefully stained to resemble driftwood found on the beach. For the walls, the designers focused on achieving a slightly darker color value to reduce the unrelenting glare from the ocean. "White paint would have been extremely harsh and unpleasant to live with," Hayes explains.

The living room, perhaps the house's most dramatic space, required close attention. The room has two window bays with stunning eyebrow window dormers, yet is large and elongated. Hayes used a large rectangular table and a custom-made chandelier to divide the room into two sitting areas, thus breaking down the room's enormous scale and creating more intimate areas for conversation. In keeping with the interior's deliberately purposeful aesthetic, Hayes designed a pair of large coffee tables for the living room, with bronze bases that are reminiscent of whalebones. Thick glass-slab tops give the edges visual softness. "The table gives weight and substance to the two seating areas and makes subtle reference to the ocean, its inhabitants, and the beach glass that my client collects on her meditative walks on the shore," says Hayes.

Like the house's interior, its exterior landscape is controlled and purposeful. The swimming pool is a strict rectangle set in a lawn surrounded by undulating hydrangea shrubs and trees. The pool and garden are below the dune line, and thus feel protected and secluded. Hayes explains that with the exception of the occasional overnight guest—and the couple's content Golden Retriever—the house is quiet and free of distractions, making it a perfect summer getaway.

*(Opposite) A sandy-gray palette with bronze and black accents evokes the atmosphere of an overcast beach day. The cast bronze base of the custom coffee table was inspired by photographs of whalebone fragments. The eighteenth-century Italian mirror is one of a pair in the living room. The Japanese black lacquer kimono storage chest, ca. 1850, is one of a mismatched pair.*

(Previous pages) A rectangular center table and custom bronze chandelier divide the elongated living room, moderating its large scale and defining two separate seating areas. The table, with an original travertine top, is a rare piece by French designer Jean-Charles Moreau.

(Above) In the dining room, dark furnishings add energy to an otherwise sedate interior. Hayes designed the dining table in statuary bronze with a stone top, and matching chairs of exposed dark wood and slate-gray leather. The limed oak sideboard is by Jean Royère, ca. 1939. (Opposite) Dramatic accents in the dining room include a pair of English Regency patinated bronze neoclassical urns and a twelve-arm Venetian chandelier of hand-blown amethyst glass, ca. 1945. The paintings are antique Chinese exports.

(Following pages) Spare rectilinear forms, including a custom-designed lacquered bed and stone and bronze side tables, create a meditative mood in the bedroom and throughout the house. The spherical Danish table lamps are ceramic on a patinated brass base, ca. 1930s.

# UPSTATE COUNTRY HOME

Westchester, New York
1996

When a pair of Hayes's clients, a couple for whom he had designed a Park Avenue apartment, asked him to work on a new country house in rural Westchester County, Hayes embarked on a detour—literally and figuratively—from his Manhattan-based portfolio. Although the new house would be built from the ground up to replace an existing 1960s house, the clients had been using the property for six years and were already intimate with the sixteen-acre site amid gently rolling hills, open meadows, and woodland, and surrounded by old stone walls and horse farms.

As Hayes approached this bucolic setting over dirt-and-gravel roads, his first impressions were cinematic. "It reminded me more of a 1940s experience of country living: commuting to and from the city, raising a family, the movie *Mr. Blandings Builds His Dream House*." The architect had conceived a house in the regional style of a turn-of-the-century New England farmhouse with additions made gradually and organically over the years. Hayes thus sought to meld elements from many decades, from the colonial era to the 1940s, into a seamless interior for modern living.

Although modern design was not called for, a modern attitude was. "I knew that it had to be visually warm, comfortable, child-friendly, and a true family retreat," says Hayes. The clients emphasized the importance of real spaces rather than showcases: a library that would provide a cozy refuge for reading, a formal dining room for entertaining, and a functional living room for socializing.

Hayes kept the family's comfort a priority as he began assembling a collection of eighteenth- and nineteenth-century antiques. To complement the house's architecture, he combined Federal antiques with English pieces. He then juxtaposed these pairings with custom furnishings that were practical and functional. In the living room, for example, the custom-made wool rug was inspired by a small, nineteenth-century American version of a hooked rug. Wing chairs flank a fireplace with a simple white mantel and stone surround; directly adjacent to the living room is a billiard room that opens off the entrance hall. As Hayes explains: "The clients and their friends play pool and hang out in this living-room area; it's not just a set made to be looked at and not used."

Neutral colors dominate throughout the house, accented with rich shades of red and blue and the burnished woods of period pieces. Walls are primarily warm gray and creamy yellow and surrounded by white moldings and doorframes. In the library, Hayes honored the classic American palette by painting the walls white, adding blue drapes, cushions, and traditional red wall sconces.

In designing this house, Hayes says, "I used a passion for things American, naïve, and handmade," which he honed years ago when he owned an 1830s farmhouse in the Catskill Mountains and developed an affinity for folk art. "My attempt to keep the choices grounded in reality was aided by this notion of a pure and simple collection of things."

*(Opposite) Mahogany cannonball beds in a guest bedroom were stained black to bring a modern emphasis on form to the traditional interior.*

*(Following pages) A nineteenth-century sideboard and gilt mirror form a welcoming tableau in the entry hall. The warm pine floors were reclaimed from a Sears & Roebuck warehouse in Chicago.*

(Previous pages) Public rooms are airy and light, with a sweeping view from the living room through the billiard room, with its restored mahogany pool table, to the entry hall beyond.

(Above) English and Federal antiques and custom pieces were combined throughout the house to create a comfortable family retreat. In the living room, deep brown curtains, dark polished wood, and a hand-hooked wool rug accent a neutral palette. (Opposite) A 360-degree mural, Tuscany on the Hudson by Stephen Hannock, surrounds the dining room in a nod to the house's location in the Hudson Valley. Deep wingback chairs flank a George III mahogany table, ca. 1800.

# WAINSCOTT SUMMER HOUSE

Wainscott, New York
1997

Countless words have been written to describe the Hamptons, mainly focusing on the area's rich artistic and agricultural history or on its more recent reputation as a magnet for celebrities and traffic. Often overlooked, however, are its serene, domestic pleasures: lovely turn-of-the-century houses and their lush gardens, washed in the incomparable light of Long Island's south shore. The owners of one such property, a shingle-style house on several acres of land in a prestigious enclave, approached Hayes for a fresh design concept that would integrate the house's breathtaking exterior with a polished, casual interior.

As two professionals committed to numerous social and cultural causes, the couple regularly entertains friends and clients. In addition to commissioning Hayes for the interiors, the couple hired an architect to unify the rooms of the main house, convert the garage into additional living quarters, and join the two structures. "This is a modern family living in the present. They don't dwell in nostalgia or sentiment," Hayes says in describing the clients. "They simply like the old rambling house, which, I think, gives them a sense of spontaneity and freedom that they don't experience in the city."

Because the family, consisting of the couple, their teenage children, and pets, had been living in the house for several years, they had a clear sense of how the rooms should function. The wife's request seemed simple: in addition to presenting a list of requirements for entertaining, "she wanted predominantly blue and white interior colors that she associated with summer and the beach," Hayes explains. "As I saw it, my design problem was to add an element that would help prevent the blue-and-white color scheme from looking too sweet, cute, and contrived." In addition, Hayes felt the design had to create a cohesive identity that would speak to the house's past, present, and future.

As a solution, he introduced dark and black furniture to provide contrast and a more serious tone that would balance the light colors in the rooms. Starting with creamy white walls and dark wood floors throughout the house, he then chose a simple collection of light, summery, durable fabrics for upholstery and window treatments. He anchored this color scheme with selected pieces of grand, black wooden furniture that call attention to the traditional ancestry of the house yet provide drama. Finally, Hayes discovered and added several mid-twentieth-century pieces crafted with eclectic materials, including Lucite, rope, steel, and whimsically carved oak. "The inclusion of industrial and twentieth-century pieces gives the house a heavier, more grounded base to build on," Hayes explains.

More than any other of the designer's projects, this house has continued to evolve. Hayes meets with his clients at the end of each summer to discuss changes and projects that they would like to accomplish by the following year, such as introducing new paint colors and replacing curtains. The owners also rotate artwork seasonally from their extensive collection. "It has been wonderful to have the opportunity to see and experience the client living in the design we created, modifying and improving it along their way in life," the designer remarks. "Plus, I get to stay in the guesthouse every now and then!"

*(Opposite) A 1950s Italian oak seashell-motif cabinet in the main entry hall is one of several mid-twentieth-century pieces selected by Hayes to energize the overall light interior.*

(Above and opposite) Creamy white walls and dark-stained wood floors dominate the color scheme throughout the house. Hayes selected light, durable upholstery, such as canvas ticking for the bobbin settee in the entry hall (above) and the open-back sofa in the living room (opposite). The custom tattersall-pattern rug repeats in several rooms; blue and white also appear in several works of art, such as this 1998 print by Terry Winters.

(Following pages) A dramatic French ebonized cupboard, ca. 1860, was the starting point for a polished new interior in this rambling beach house. Hayes added several black period pieces to the requested blue-and-white palette to establish a more serious tone. Slipcovers in light, natural fabrics keep the living room casual. A pair of Hayes-designed bobbin chairs flanks the fireplace; the antique American floor lamps are bronze with milk-glass shades.

(Opposite) The dining room includes a French ebonized console table and an unusual set of steel Windsor chairs originally used in a nineteenth-century meeting hall. The forged iron chandelier is Spanish, ca. 1920. (Above) The broad, shady porch of the shingle-style house is used frequently for outdoor entertaining. The porch connects the house to the sweeping front lawn and once served as the passage to the main entry door.

*(Above and opposite) In a bedroom off the sunroom, Hayes combined traditional American and English antiques, such as an English mahogany four-poster bed, with eclectic modern pieces. The chest of drawers (right) contains Hepplewhite-style drawers in a modern Lucite case. The mercury glass bedside lamps are Italian, from the 1940s.*

# CONTEMPORARY ART COLLECTORS APARTMENT

New York, New York
2002

For this spacious apartment with East River views, Hayes was commissioned by a long-time client, a well-traveled couple who are passionate collectors of contemporary art, to conceive an updated scheme that would respect the existing architecture and design while accommodating their expanding art collection and changing family needs. Many years earlier, the client had worked with the renowned late decorator Jed Johnson and the architect Alan Wanzenberg on the original interior. "They had designed a handsome apartment, which made my job that much nicer," says Hayes, who had been friends with Johnson and maintains great respect for his work. "We were not dismantling his design but completing it and changing pieces that were placeholders."

Programmatically, several of the apartment's five rooms required rethinking since the clients' children were now in college and no longer living at home; yet the space still had to accommodate large family meals and entertaining for groups of friends and philanthropic causes. Addressing these needs, Hayes decided to create two new seating areas in the living room and provide plenty of space for standing and conversation.

On an aesthetic level, Hayes recalls, "They wanted the apartment to reflect old-world elegance, which the building exudes, but they also wanted it to feel younger and more upbeat, yet not trendy or too 'of the moment.'" This attitude, not coincidentally, dovetailed with Hayes's

own design philosophy: "Good design can be inspired by popular culture and fashion, but shouldn't derive shape and form directly from current trends," he maintains. He first simplified the color scheme, freshening several of the main rooms with a subdued gray and brown palette. Further unifying the interior, he then reupholstered most of the existing furniture in the same neutral fabric, with the exception of a new sofa. The custom-mixed deep blue paint of the dining room, on the other hand, is reminiscent of Park Avenue apartments of the 1940s and 1950s and presents a rich contrast to the other main rooms.

"The principal idea here was to create a richness in the materials, fabrics, rugs, and found furniture that felt appropriate for such a grand and elegant apartment, and at the same time made it neutral enough to accommodate a variety of art that is always changing," Hayes explains. A living-room table was replaced with a taller custom cabinet with a graphic motif that relates well to the artwork. Likewise, in the hallway, Hayes installed picture shelves at two levels that give the client multiple display options.

The overall result is a calm, cohesive environment that affords the client newfound possibilities. As Hayes characterizes it: "Nothing is startling or extreme, yet the experience is never mundane." The apartment, he feels, "strikes a pleasant, easy visual chord that suggests a high level of style and sophistication without overly dramatic or pretentious overtones."

*(Opposite) Six woodcuts from a series of ten by Donald Judd (1988), French chairs from the 1940s, and a custom mahogany table create a modern study in geometry and pattern in the dining room. Hayes worked with color consultants to formulate an unusual deep blue wall color evocative of lead-based prewar paint. A Venetian chandelier hangs above the table.*

(Above) A Venetian lamp and Swedish mahogany table in an intimate corner seating area introduce a smaller scale to the expansive living room. On the wall is a panel in graphite by Frank Gerritz, Between the Lines (Parallel Universe IV) (2002). (Opposite) A saturated palette in the living room creates a neutral background for the clients' collection of contemporary art, yet it also respects the elegant prewar architecture. A Donald Judd construction contrasts with the curved lines of the chairs, the piano, and a late-1930s torchère lamp by Tommi Parzinger.

*(Above) The traditional dining room, with a Venetian chandelier and deep blue walls, combines elements of an elegant Parisian apartment with modern furniture and art. Matching mahogany-top tables with brass bases were custom-designed to provide seating for both large-scale entertaining and intimate breakfasts overlooking the East River. In the foreground is a marble torso by Bruno Mankowski (1938).*

(Previous pages) The strong geometry of a 1930 Borsani sideboard adds a modernist focus to the traditional, romantic living room. The careful, asymmetrical arrangement of contemporary art and furniture enlivens the room. Ann Hamilton's photograph Reflection (12:40) (1999/2000) hangs above the sideboard, counterbalanced by a sculptural head in pigmented grout by Michael Ferris (2005).

(Above) An etching by Damien Hirst, Twist and Shout (1992), hangs in the dining room above a French fruit-wood cabinet from the 1940s. Traditional accessories include an English mahogany tray with silver tea service and a 1930s Swiss clock. (Opposite) A compact, mahogany-top table and leather armchairs by Louis Sognot from the late 1920s create a romantic breakfast seating area with a river view.

# DUNE HOUSE

Watermill, New York
2007

While Hayes counts several beach houses among his projects, this one—a modern, flat-roofed, wood and glass house for an existing client—is a milestone for him, one he feels ideally represents his modernist sensibility and desire for pared-down clarity. "There's an economy to it," Hayes says of the two-story house, which lies on a thin spit of land between Long Island's Mecox Bay and the Atlantic Ocean. Light, air, and a close connection to nature were the guiding themes of the project. Broad glass doors in all of the rooms open to views of the bay on one side and views of the dunes and ocean on the other. But, says Hayes, the house is "less about the views out of the rooms, and more about harmoniously drawing the textures, palette, and organic forms of nature into the rooms."

Hayes knew the clients well, having designed their residence in Manhattan and winter home in Park City, Utah. "I knew they didn't care for overwrought design, self-conscious moves, and 'of the moment' gestures," he says. With two children of high school and college age who surf and swim, "they wanted an easy summer house that they could live in now and as they got older, without worrying about eating and sitting on the furniture after a day at the beach."

Over many months, Hayes collaborated with the architect to select finishes, hardware, and lighting, and he designed most of the furniture specifically for the house. Comfortable custom pieces are upholstered in durable cottons and linens, and nearly all of the fabric incorporates synthetic material for easy maintenance. Area rugs, too, are vinyl, so they can be mopped clean. In the family room, even the coffee table top is covered in sturdy fabric, inviting the family and guests to put up their feet.

Yet while the clients did not want a precious, delicate interior, they do collect art and appreciate refined objects. The first thing Hayes purchased for the house, in fact, was a six-foot-diameter Austrian chandelier that adds an unexpected note of luxury and elegance to the enormous, double-height living room, with its two simple seating arrangements. Classic mid-twentieth-century furniture by Edward Wormley, Ward Bennet, Mies van der Rohe, and Pierre Jeanneret honor the house's modernist influences. "It's an important project for me because it still incorporates found things. I still like that discovery and hunt—it's an exciting component."

Hayes also felt strongly that found pieces should speak to origins that are directly associated with nature and its organic, tactile qualities. "You see a table and think tree," Hayes offers. "See a chair and think of the soft, sensuous curves of wood found on the beach. You might look at a painting and imagine a waterfall, or at another work of art that is visually similar to the texture of tree bark." As a result, rooms throughout the house contain a focused selection of unique found pieces crafted of beautiful wood—many of them by midcentury Japanese-American designer and architect George Nakashima, as well as noted Brazilian artist Sergio Rodriguez.

The dining room, for example, is a simple volume containing a custom wood table, Brazilian jacaranda wood chairs, and a custom server with oak doors carved in a pattern that suggests rippling water. A "school" of abstract ceramic fish plates in shimmering shades of off-white, gray, and charcoal floats across one wall.

On the second floor, an open bridge connects the master bedroom to a work and reading area with its own deck overlooking the ocean. Hayes positioned armchairs in the master bedroom to face Mecox Bay, a view he considers more reflective and serene than the ocean view. Furnishings in the bedrooms reinforce the minimal approach: custom platform beds, reading areas, and simple desks and chairs. Hayes feels the interiors are particularly relevant today, when broader cultural concerns stress economy over excess, and respect for the natural environment. "I think it's reflective of contemporary family living," he says of the house. "The result for the family is a place of quiet, reflective solitude. Symbiosis between man and nature, or harmony with nature, becomes the perfect summer escape from city living."

*(Opposite) Simplicity, light, and a close connection to nature define the interior. Organic found pieces, such as a pequi wood table by a Brazilian artist, complement custom furniture upholstered in durable fabrics.*

*(Previous pages) Two seating areas define the double-height living room, with views to the dunes. A 1950s "Sputnik" chandelier found in a Viennese theater adds a note of luxury and refinement.*

*(Above) A pair of rare midcentury teak and cotton-upholstered chairs by Pierre Jeanneret flanks a side table by Paul Evans and Phillip Powell. (Opposite) The living room opens to the entry hall and a second-floor sitting room/workspace.*

*(Opposite) Sunlight floods the living room, energizing a subtle palette. A large-scale painting by Hawaiian artist Tadashi Sato, Untitled (Nakalele) (1983), is a vivid focal point. The late-1940s iron table lamp is by Tommi Parzinger. (Above) Limestone floor slabs and cedar paneling connect the entry hall with the exterior, and 1960s ceramic pots from the Architectural Pottery Company complement the spare aesthetic. The painting by Pat Steir, Two White Whistling (2006), suggests the fluidity of a waterfall.*

(Previous pages) Window sheers centered on broad glass doors form the backdrop to a custom server and a collection of midcentury vases by Swedish designer Berndt Friberg. Dining chairs in jacaranda wood by Brazilian designer Joaquim Tenreiro, ca. 1960, surround the custom table.

(Above) The focus of the dining room is a collection of hand-painted abstract ceramic fish plates by the Southern California–based artist La Gardo Tackett, ca. 1950. (Opposite) Cerused oak doors on the custom server emulate the effect of rippling water and add to a heightened awareness of texture throughout the house.

(Following pages) Custom furniture in the family room is upholstered in a sturdy, nubby linen suitable for indoor-outdoor living. The pair of fossil lamps flanking the sofa is by French designers Charles Moreau and Bolette Natanson, ca. 1930–1935; the lithograph is by Ellsworth Kelly.

(Above) The family room features a custom-designed punee, or traditional Hawaiian daybed, and a set of Mies van der Rohe Brno chairs, ca. 1960, with new slipcovers. The hanging wall case and floor lamp are by George Nakashima. (Opposite) Next to the quilted daybed is a mid-1960s ash side table with laminated tray top by Edward Wormley.

(Following pages) A bridge on the second floor leads from the master bedroom to the sitting room, with doors opening to ocean views. The white lacquer custom cabinet houses a television and office equipment.

*(Above) Large windows and minimal details in the master bathroom emphasize luminous views of the bay and landscape surrounding the house. (Opposite) In the master bedroom, two high-back armchairs and matching ottomans by Edward Wormley face Mecox Bay, a view that emphasizes serene reflection. Between the chairs is a walnut table with burlwood handle by George Nakashima.*

(Opposite) A custom oak-and-upholstered headboard with built-in night tables in the large master bedroom separates the sleeping area from the reading area behind it. (Above) Hayes designed the bedrooms as quiet, meditative spaces, with custom platform beds and quilted bedcovers. Here, found pieces include a walnut bedside cabinet by George Nakashima, ca. 1960, and a Danish chair from the 1950s.

(Following pages) On the lower level, a yoga/fitness room overlooks a Japanese-inspired walled rock garden. A Noguchi paper lantern and upholstered "boulders" invite relaxation and conversation.

A LIFE IN DESIGN

THAD HAYES

My interest in the visual arts was first encouraged in the early 1960s, when my mother enrolled me in an art class held at the Sears department store in Baton Rouge, Louisiana. I had been doing a lot of drawing in grade school, and perhaps she thought that I might have talent. More likely, as a full-time math teacher in the Baton Rouge public school system, a homemaker, and the single parent of three small boys, she simply needed to park me somewhere for a couple of hours when I was not at school. An art class, happily, was one of her choices for me.

Southern Louisiana at that time offered little in the way of cultural opportunities in the conventional sense—museums and the theater were practically non-existent—but it was steeped in history, and looking at buildings became part of my visual education. Every few months my mother would plan a Sunday trip to visit historic houses, gardens, and towns in the region, including the great plantation houses: Rosedown, Oak Alley, Oakley (most famously the one-time home of the wildlife artist John Audubon), and many more. We would prepare a picnic, load up the Oldsmobile, and be off on our journey.

Historic preservation, as it is known today, was not a very strong concern in the 1960s when we visited these houses, and only their existence as tourist attractions saved them from the fate of better-known landmarks like New York's original Pennsylvania Station. Many of these properties were either completely open to the public or partially open, with private, owner-occupied wings and zones. At that time, there was little money to maintain them, and their furnishing tended to be incomplete and not true to the house's historic period. Yet I would not have loved them and learned as much from them had their interiors been appointed as completely as, for example, those at the country estate Winterthur, in Delaware, with its rigorous historical correctness. The lack of much furniture in these historic Southern homes—and the absence of window treatments, rugs, and works of art—revealed the architecture itself as simple, minimal, and beautiful. I remember these threadbare interiors as rich and complete, and the fully and properly furnished interiors I try to create today are as spare and uncrowded as I can make them.

Along the routes to the plantations, we drove through magnificent, sweeping, flat landscapes—levees, rivers, lakes, and long allées of oaks. I will always remember the huge, splendid oaks on either side of the drive connecting Oak Alley to the Mississippi River. The planting of these trees nearly three hundred years ago was a man-made gesture of immense aesthetic power, as were the simply and boldly designed levee and spillway systems and the bridges of the region.

Our own home, in a very small, rural town in south-central Louisiana, was continually fixed and upgraded by my parents. My mother liked designing things for it and was an avid reader and collector of decorating and architecture magazines. She also gardened and put my brothers and me to work digging, weeding, hoeing, planting, and pruning. In the late 1950s she and my father added a large living room in the then-current modernist style, a strong contrast to our more traditional existing house. I remember being excited by its jalousie windows, Hardoy butterfly chairs, platform sofas, and matchstick roller blinds, all quite new to me.

My father and mother divorced when I was young. My father was a hardworking, blue-collar man who drove a tow truck. He was often irascible, with a tough exterior, yet he was generous, well-liked, and widely known in town. He was also very private: his aesthetic, sensitive qualities were known to few. What was

*(Opposite) Shared offices of designers Robert Bray and Michael Schaible (Bray-Schaible Design), and Joseph D'Urso, Bryant Park Studios, New York, 1977. Currently the office of Thad Hayes, Inc.*

eccentric and perhaps even bizarre about him, however, was his hobby: collecting good English, American, and Chinese antiques—lots of them—which he managed to do well despite having no formal training. He wasn't the sort to go to New Orleans and buy something retail. Instead, in the evening, after his day on the tow truck, he would often go to someone's home to look at a piece. I believe his main interest was genuinely in old, beautiful things—in the antiques themselves, rather than the money he made off them. He kept most of what he collected, only periodically selling to a few private customers. His home after the divorce was very modest, and its interior was more like a warehouse than a home. It was crammed full of things hanging from the walls and piled on tables and chairs, and there was no place to sit. By the time I was in college and had taken some history of art and architecture courses, I knew that his collection was really good. Later in his life, while continuing to buy antiques, he began to collect huge, heavy objects like ships' anchors and other quirky things.

If it was my good fortune to have a father with an unlikely and perhaps extreme passion for the decorative arts, I was also lucky as a child to be able to observe the everyday building of ordinary houses. When I was quite young my mother's only sister, Aunt Marietta, and her husband began planning a new, modern house designed by a New Orleans architect. Seeing the blue-

prints at the age of five greatly impressed me; I remember admiring the fine white lines on the field of blue. I was fascinated that someone had actually planned the house and made the drawings so that a builder could put it up, and I watched the entire process, from the pouring of the slab to the construction of the walls and roof. The interior designer selected primarily Danish modern furniture manufactured in the late 1950s. The upholstery was sleek and modern; off-white, beige, and chocolate brown dominated; "tangerine orange" and aqua blue were used sparingly for accents such as throw pillows; and, in the dining room, a large niche was lacquered orange for the display of china. The whole look was new, fresh, and snappy.

When I was five we moved to Baton Rouge, into a house in a partially built subdivision. With the city still in the midst of the postwar housing boom, hundreds of acres of open meadows and wooded fields nearby were available for construction, and four or five new houses were always underway within a short distance from our house. By the time I was nine I would visit these sites on my bike when the workmen were away, sneaking into the houses to study the layouts and see where and how materials were applied. Most of the houses were traditional—a mix of postwar ranch style with a little French Quarter romanticism thrown in—but on rare occasions a very decent modern house would appear, complete with clerestories, walled entry courts, and terrazzo floors.

*(Opposite left) Oakley Plantation House, St. Francisville, Louisiana, 1799–1806. (Opposite right) Wells House, Natchitoches, Louisiana, late 1770s. (Right) Ward Bennett House, East Hampton, New York, 1970s.*

In the mid-1960s my mother hired a professional decorator and invited me to sit in on all the meetings. He brought fabric books and furniture catalogs, and I began to hear decorators' small talk. I remember that he wore a dark suit and bright tie and drove a black Lincoln Continental—the first clue for me that interior design could be an actual business and not just my mother's hobby. Nevertheless, my decision to make it a career was a long time coming.

I attended the Louisiana State University School of Environmental Design with the intention of pursuing the five-year bachelor of architecture degree, but I had graduated from high school at the end of the first semester of my senior year, and the freshman architectural program didn't begin until fall. The five-year landscape architecture program was open, however, and I signed up with the idea of switching to architecture later. As it turned out, I stayed with landscape design for the entire five years, because the teachers were excellent and very contemporary in their thinking, and I admired the rigorous way they taught concepts applicable to the design of anything—a knife and fork, a garden, a building, a chair.

With my landscape architecture degree in hand, I moved to New York. It was January 1979, the country was in recession, and I didn't even try to get a job before I came to the city. I found occasional small-scale design jobs with firms that were still doing terraces, townhouse and penthouse gardens, and rooftops. My first important project was working with Tim DuVal, a landscape designer, to design Robert De Niro's rooftop in Tribeca. In those years, fortunately, it was still possible for a young person to be poor, live in Manhattan, have a good time, and eat well.

As I worked, these little exterior projects began to seem more like interior spaces, and all the knowledge and interest I had in architecture began to come into play. High-tech, minimalist, low-budget interior design—as practiced in New York by Joseph Paul D'Urso, Robert Bray and Michael Schaible, the late Ward Bennett, and others—excited me because they were using inexpensive products—surgical glass containers, laboratory and industrial surfaces and finishes—in fresh and original ways. Just as important, I was meeting people who lived in lofts with very minimal, elegant, and serene spaces, a look with which I was not familiar. Seeing all this finally pulled me into interior design.

In June, 1979, I rented a raw, empty, 1,200-square-foot loft on Twenty-seventh Street. Even though it was on a high floor, with a view of the Empire State Building, no one wanted such a space at that time, so it was very cheap. My design for the loft was a direct reaction to published photographs of Robert Bray's studio apartment. Bray's walls were glossy white, his floors cov-

ered with charcoal gray industrial carpeting. Gray tones were used everywhere else, and the effect was minimalist. As it happened, the painter and designer Stephen Shadley lived upstairs, and sometime after I had completed my new home he introduced me to Bray. Bob saw my loft and liked it; we became good friends, and he encouraged me to move from landscape architecture to interior design. In December of that year I flew back to Baton Rouge for the holidays, and at the airport I bought a copy of *Architectural Digest* because it featured one of Bray's projects. Coincidentally, my mother greeted me with the news that he had called, and when we spoke he invited me to work for him and Michael Schaible. His offer not only made my Christmas—it launched my career.

The Bray and Schaible office was located in Bryant Park Studios, a beautiful ten-story Beaux-Arts building facing the park between Fortieth and Forty-second streets, directly behind the New York Public Library. The building was designed by Charles A. Rich in 1901 as a place for visual artists to work and live. When I think of all the possible workplaces I might have found myself in at the beginning of my life in New York, it seems a most generous gift of fate that I should have begun those days in a portion of Midtown so rich in architecture, art, design, and their history. The studios in the building are amazing double-height spaces, with large windows to capture the unobstructed north

light above the park. Generations of distinguished artists had maintained studios and been residents in the building, among them Edward Steichen and Fernand Léger. Irving Penn had his photography studio there in the 1950s, and in 1977, Bray and Schaible leased that same studio.

I worked for Bob as an assistant in the true sense—obtaining orders and samples, shopping, gathering images, reviewing drawings, and accompanying him on photo shoots. Not yet a junior designer, I learned a tremendous amount just by being present in the office and watching everything Bray did. An often-overlooked aspect of this business is that interior designers are not always fortunate enough to have handsome architectural interiors to enhance. Instead, we are sometimes given mediocre spaces with low ceilings, cramped rooms, and little light. Bray was a master at taking an ordinary apartment, clearing out unnecessary walls, and inserting grand doors that reached the ceiling and walls that pivot to open or enclose adjoining spaces. He played with scale in ways that helped create a strong architectural statement when there was no strong architecture. All of his work was elegant, simple, and modern.

After three years with Bray and Schaible, I came to think that I had learned enough to start my own firm. Sometimes ignorance is bliss. I was young and fearless and had no idea what the future held for me. I

(Opposite left) Philip Johnson, Glass House, New Canaan, Connecticut, 1949. (Opposite right) Robert Bray apartment, New York, 1978. (Right) Thad Hayes at home with his son Daniel in 2008.

had secured a single project to start my own business, but this project ended just one month after it began. I was patient and waited a couple of months; then, in 1985, I rented a little office at 160 Fifth Avenue, near Twenty-first Street, with a desk and phone. Around this time I met Terry Wilke, co-owner of the menswear company Wilke-Rodriguez, who commissioned two new projects from me. I went on to design a large two-floor space for his company that was widely published. Wilke was a wonderful first client, and very supportive of my efforts. During those early years, Robert Bray also referred small jobs to me, and soon I was able to move my office to a duplex loft space in Tribeca.

Much of the work in this book was completed over the course of thirteen years in that relatively compact space. In 2003 I had the good luck to relocate my office to the same quarters once held by Bray and Schaible in Bryant Park Studios. The large windows facing the park allow me to pay attention to the way people enjoy that great public space of New York. Because I design for people, I also observe how they move, react, play, and function in their homes. I still love to look at houses—both important historical examples and simple generic structures. Everything from cliff dwellings to Monticello interests me, as well as many styles—colonial, Arts and Crafts, art deco, southwest adobe, farmhouses, and barns.

My home is now in a suburb of New York that is a better place to rear my young son, but I will always be fascinated by the city. As many New Yorkers attest, the place is a magnet that draws one back into its energy field. I have come full circle, back to the workplace where I started, practicing an art of which my mother and father were my first teachers, and Robert Bray the best of all possible mentors.

I am grateful, first and foremost, to all those individuals whom I have had the pleasure of working with—and working for—since opening my studio doors in 1985. A particular debt of gratitude is due to those committed, determined, and patient clients who willingly subjected themselves to the long, and often arduous, process of creating a new home. In my line of work it is easy to begin believing one is laboring for one's art. My humble thanks to all those clients, craftsmen, architects, and employees who gently reminded me—on such occasions when I lost sight of the fact—that interior design is a service business.

A heartfelt thanks to my family, who encouraged, usually without question, my pursuit of art and design in all forms: my Aunt Marietta, my brothers Lance and Paul, my father and especially my mother, Elaine.

To my clients, who have been willing and accepting of my direction and ideas, I express my great appreciation and fondness. My heartfelt thanks to those clients who have particularly supported my work throughout many years and with multiple projects: Laura Donnelley, Marty and David Hamamoto, Evelyn and Leonard Lauder, Karen and William Lauder, and Brooke and Daniel Neidich.

None of these projects would have been realized without the talented contractors, upholsterers, furniture makers, antique dealers, and consultants with whom I've worked for twenty-three years. To these seldom-mentioned, incredibly skilled, tremendously creative, legion of artisans, craftsmen, and artists I offer my deepest respect. Thank you all for so generously sharing your knowledge, insights, and passion for all things related to construction and design. I am an apprentice to you all.

To all my teachers, mentors, and closest friends, who continue to inspire me, thank you ever so much. I especially thank my mentor Robert Bray; also Michael Schaible, Jon Emerson, Wayne Womack, Lurline Lemieux, and Ronald McCoy; and my friends Stephen Shadley, Doug Reed, Cee Brown, David Mendoza, Robert and Lisha Sherman, and Jane Widas.

To the many magazine and book editors who have published my work, especially Paige Rense of *Architectural Digest*, who has continued to champion and encourage me: I sincerely appreciate all that you have done. Also, for their support over the years: Margaret Dunne, Charles Gandee, James Huntington, Jeffrey Nemeroff, Nancy Novogrod, Marian McEvoy, Suzanne Slesin, and Pilar Viladas.

A huge thanks to gifted photographer and friend Scott Frances, who is responsible for most of the images in this book.

Thanks to those at Rizzoli International Publications who were so patient, understanding, and kind throughout the process of making this book: David Morton, Douglas Curran, and Dung Ngo. To Mildred Schmertz, who was so helpful with editing my story, "A Life in Design." To Megan McFarland, who tirelessly edited the project descriptions and captions; and to Evelyn Lauder for writing such a warm foreword. And special thanks to Charles Gandee for his exhaustive research and interviews and for writing a fine introductory essay, "The Tailored Interior." To Renée Cologne in my office for her patience, organization, and help in coordinating all aspects of assembling this book. To everyone at Thad Hayes, Inc., past and present, who worked so hard to create and produce the work, especially Trisha Eliott, Donald Blender, Shawn Henderson, John Gachot, and friend and consultant Keith Granet.

Lastly, thank you to my partner Adam Lippin, who keeps me balanced and centered in the midst of the self-involvement that is part of the fabric of the creative mind, and to Daniel, our dear son, who is teaching me to be less selfish and more patient.

T. H.

## Photo Credits

All projects photography © Scott Frances, except:

page 12: © Colleen Duffley Photography; pages 30–35: David Glomb; pages 68-75: Michael Mundy; page 167: John M. Hall; pages 168–70: Colleen Duffley Photography; page 171: John M. Hall; page 232: © Peter Aaron/Esto. All rights reserved. 1979; page 234, left: Alex Demyan Photo, provided by Louisiana Office of State Parks; page 234, right: © Philip Gould; page 235: © P e t e r Aaron/Esto. All rights reserved. 1978; page 236, left: Paul Rocheleau Photographer ©1994; page 236, right: Jaime Ardiles-Arce.

First published in the United States of America in 2009 by
RIZZOLI INTERNATIONAL PUBLICATIONS, INC.
300 Park Avenue South
New York, NY 10010
www.rizzoliusa.com

ISBN-13: 978-0-8478-3081-7
Library of Congress Control Number: 2008937198

Distributed to the U.S. trade by Random House, New York

Designed by NGOstudio

Printed and bound in China

2009 2010 2011 2012 2013/ 10 9 8 7 6 5 4 3 2 1

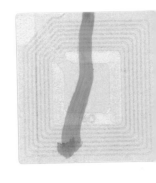